Contents

Left: The female Red-tailed Black-Cockatoo is recognisable by her yellow spots.

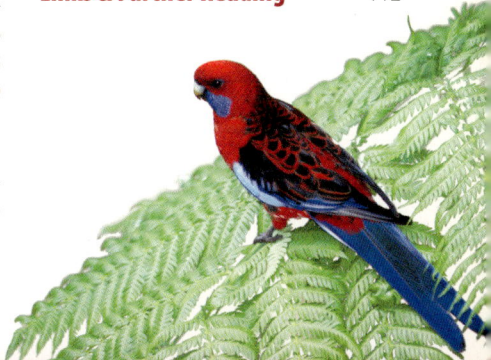

Introduction

More than 330 parrot species inhabit our planet, and Australia is home to about 56 of them. In fact, this continent's abundance of these birds led mapmakers of the 1500s to annotate the coast of a great southern land with *Psittacorum Regio* — "The Region of Parrots" — as reported by Portuguese sailing expeditions.

Australian parrots all belong to the Psittaciformes order, within which birds can be divided into three families. Cockatoos, in the Cacatuidae family, are the largest, and DNA studies have shown them to be genetically distinct from other parrots. They are characterised by solid bodies, powerful grasping claws and well-defined, movable crests. By far the majority of Australian parrots (up to 60% of Australia's species) belong to the Psittacidae family of "typical parrots". Lorikeets, in the Loriidae subfamily, have a number of biological differences that set them apart from their Psittacidae relatives. As specialist nectar-eaters, lorikeets have modified tongues with long papillae that create a brush-like texture to soak up the sugary nectar and pollen.

Defining features of all parrots are their strong, deeply down-curved bills. The upper mandible moves while the lower mandible is fitted neatly within the closed bill and has less movement. This oral structure allows parrots to manipulate seeds in the mouth, using the upper beak and flexible tongue, while holding the nut casing firmly in the bottom jaw — sometimes with the help of their deft claws. Parrots' feet are also characteristic of this group of birds. The "zygodactylous" arrangement of toes — two pointing forwards and two pointing backwards — bestows parrots with relatively nimble movement in the treetops. All the toes terminate in long, sharply curved claws, which give parrots an extremely strong grip for clinging and clambering up tree trunks and grasping slippery nuts and seedpods. This combination of beak and toe arrangement is unique to the Psittaciformes order.

Like the feathers of all birds, a parrot's feathers are made up of a protein called keratin, which is the same substance that forms human hair and fingernails.

Left: A male Eclectus Parrot shows off his powerful curved beak — the upper section of which is specialised for cracking tough seeds while the lower jaw holds them in position.

Feathers become brittle and tatty over time, despite constant preening, so parrots and cockatoos must still moult and regrow their feathers at least once a year. The primary wing feathers are shed sequentially from the middle of the wing outwards to the tip, to allow the birds to continue to fly for as long as possible while moulting. Preening, or running the beak along the shaft of the feather, enables the bird to "zip" into place the barbules that make up the vanes of the feather. Parrots also have powder-down feathers whose tips, when preened, break down into flakes of keratin. This powder coats the other feathers and keeps them sleek.

FEATURES OF A PARROT (CACATUIDAE)

Ear coverts often faintly tinted

Powder down feathers on the belly

Crest (unique to cockatoos among the Psittaciformes)

Nostrils encased in cere

Sharp, curved beak for prising open nuts and seedpods

Underwing coverts show a flash of colour during flight

Powerful zygodactylous feet for gripping branches

Undertail coverts

Primary flight feathers

Secondary flight feathers

Above: Major Mitchell's Cockatoo is one of the most brightly coloured cockatoo species. **Top:** A Rainbow Lorikeet preens its feathers; The Cockatiel is the smallest of the cockatoos and is resplendent with its bright yellow crest and red cheeks.

Seeing Parrots in the Wild

Australia's geographical isolation has allowed its parrot species to diversify across this vast continent with little competition from other large, herbivorous birds. Consequently, parrots are often seen in almost all Australian habitats, from the dry, seasonally grassy inland to the coast. Despite their bright plumage, many species are remarkably well-camouflaged in their chosen habitats, with only a flash of underwing vibrance to give them away. Only two species, the Ground Parrot and the Night Parrot, have evolved to favour a terrestrial lifestyle. Others, such as the Mulga Parrot and Rock Parrot, show a preference for specific habitats (Mulga woodlands and harsh saline dunes respectively). Rainforest species include the spectacularly large Palm Cockatoo and brilliantly coloured, sexually dimorphic Eclectus Parrot. Parrots seldom migrate, although some follow the flowering of plants which, by their feeding, they pollinate. One of the most widespread species is the Galah, which ranges across the entire mainland and Tasmania. Rosellas, which have genetically distinct representatives in each Australian State, are also extremely abundant and commonly encountered members of the parrot family.

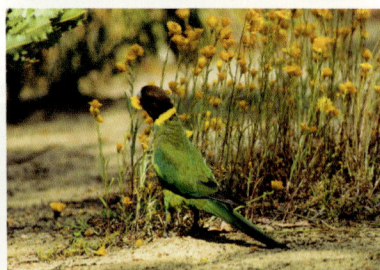

Top, left to right: A flock of Galahs wheel over the grassy interior around Flinders Ranges, South Australia; Rainforest parrots, such as the female (left) and male (right) Eclectus Parrot blend in with the colours of rainforest fruit and leaves. **Bottom, left to right:** Crimson Rosellas, shown here in the misty Bunya Mountains, are able to withstand the cooler climate of the southern States, but are not found in Tasmania, where the Green Rosella reigns; Australian Ringnecks take a number of different races. The Port Lincoln Parrot race is excellently camouflaged against the stalks and flowers of its favoured dry woodlands.

Most parrots are specialist seed-eaters that tear apart seedpods, pine cones and nuts as well as eating grass seeds and young shoots; however, some, particularly lorikeets, also consume nectar and pollen. Although most parrots remain largely herbivorous, some supplement a diet of seeds and nuts with insects and their larvae, which are often prised from beneath bark. Many subtropical and tropical species also eat fruit such as bananas, rainforest fruit and native figs. Among seed-eaters, competition is usually low as species of seed-bearing plants often produce their bounty at the same time each year, making food plentiful even when an entire flock is foraging together. Cockatoos especially benefit from a flock social structure. They cleverly post a sentry in a nearby tree to watch over the flock and alert them to danger.

A DAY IN THE LIFE...

Parrots follow a well-established day-to-day routine. Unlike some other bird species, they require water daily and usually flock to waterholes at dawn, where they drink, bathe and preen. "Breakfast" follows and the flock moves to feeding grounds a few kilometres away from watering places. Most species forage in two daily sessions, retiring mid-morning to the shelter of the treetops to wait out the hottest part of the day, then flying in to feed again in the cool of the afternoon. Parrots are diurnal (day-active birds). By night they roost communally in the treetops, often visiting the waterhole again at dusk before settling to their roost.

Right, top to bottom: Rainbow Lorikeets are nectarivores; Mulga Parrots forage on the ground for seeds; Orchardists and fruit growers are often visited by Australian King-Parrots; A Sulphur-crested Cockatoo uses its feet to steady its meal; Most parrots, such as these Galahs, use a "dip and tilt" method to drink, but some cockatoos have been observed slurping through an angled beak.

The Parrot Life Cycle

Most parrots and cockatoos pair for life and renew their attraction with mutual preening and "courtship feeding" — whereby the male offers his partner gifts of food during the breeding season. When attracting a female, male parrots may swivel their heads, pirouette, preen the female and nibble at her head and beak. Male cockatoos frequently bob their heads up and down and raise and lower their crests. Spring is the preferred breeding time for many cockatoo and parrot species. One to six eggs are laid on consecutive days, with the number of eggs determined by the particular species. Some species do not incubate the eggs until all are laid, so that all the chicks hatch together; others begin to incubate from the first egg, so hatching is staggered. Nests are usually situated deep in hollows, either inside a large bough or deep within the trunk of a tall tree. A lining of chips of eucalypt bark, gum leaves or chewed-up twigs helps protect the eggs and chicks. Exceptions to this are the ground-dwelling species, which include the Night Parrot, Ground Parrot and Rock Parrot. The Rock Parrot does not make a nest at all, preferring to lay eggs in a shallow depression on a rocky ledge or coastal cliff-face.

A HOLLOW FEELING

Studies have shown that eggs laid in tree hollows and cavities are statistically safer than those laid in stick nests; however, a tree hollow home has its own disadvantages. Hollows can be extremely hard to come by. Most parrots use the same hollow year after year and are extremely territorial. Because hollows usually only form in large, old trees, competition for nest spaces is tight. Unfortunately, deforestation and land clearing have reduced the availability of avian nest sites. Some species, such as white cockatoos, usually share incubation of the eggs, which takes about 30 days, but in black-cockatoo species only the female incubates the eggs. While the female broods the eggs in the hollow, her partner brings her food.

Left: A pair of Rainbow Lorikeets in their hollow.
Top: Mutual preening helps strengthen the pair bond for these two Yellow-tailed Black-Cockatoos.

Top, left to right: Sulphur-crested Cockatoos nest in hollows high in eucalypts, where their eggs and chicks are protected from most threats apart from goannas, snakes, other birds and deforestation; A pair of Purple-crowned Lorikeets loiter near the mouth of their nesting hollow. **Bottom, left to right:** Galahs nest inside a long tunnel in a hollow and line their nest with a layer of gum leaves; All parrots lay white eggs, but this might not be as advantageous for the Ground Parrot, whose eggs are laid into a round mass of grasses and are more vulnerable to predation by terrestrial predators. Most ground-laying birds have speckled eggs.

BIRD NURSERIES

All parrots lay white, only slightly oblong eggs. Because many parrots nest in tree hollows, their eggs are hidden from view and do not require speckling for camouflage. In the darkness of the hollow, the white eggs are also easier for the parents to see. Because nests in tree hollows are snug and secure, parrots' eggs do not need to be oval-shaped as they are unable to roll out of the nest anyway. When the chicks hatch, they are blind and mostly featherless. Feathers usually start to grow at around four weeks, but are frequently paler than the adults' plumage and remain sheathed for some time. Most chicks stay in the nest for 5–6 weeks. However, hatchlings of some species remain dependent on their parents for a further 4–6 weeks after leaving the nest and may be left in a "creche" with other juveniles while the parents seek food. Once independent, juvenile birds often form wandering flocks until they form a pair bond.

People & Parrots

Most people are delighted when they encounter parrots flying free in their natural environment; however, most of the interaction between people and these spectacular birds occurs in backyards, camping grounds, suburban parks or aviaries. Many parrot species appear almost unafraid of humans and can become quite tame around places where humans and birds cohabit. Because they are flocking birds, it is not unusual for campers to be besieged by scores of chattering lorikeets alighting on their heads and outstretched arms at campsites. Although parrots can easily be enticed to take food from humans or visit a backyard birdfeeder, it is important to ensure that, firstly, the food being given is appropriate and, secondly, that only small amounts are given so that the birds do not become reliant on humans for food. Giving parrots the wrong kind of food can damage their beaks and affect their health. A better way to attract parrots, particularly lorikeets, is to plant a native garden using seed-bearing or nectar-producing plants. Birdbaths also attract some species, such as gregarious Rainbow Lorikeets and Crimson Rosellas.

PARROTS AS PETS

Since Europeans first settled Australia, the continent's most admired and colourful parrot species have attracted the attention of aviarists and pet-lovers. Parrots are intelligent, affectionate animals that are able to exist on a simple vegetarian diet of seeds, fruit and plants, making them excellent and easy-to-care-for pets. Two of Australia's native parrots, Cockatiels and Budgerigars, are now widely regarded as some of the world's most popular avian pets and have been bred in captivity to create numerous variations in colour and plumages. All parrots kept as pets should have access to large enclosures or flying spaces, natural sunlight, nest hollows and plenty of fresh food and water. Some larger species, such as cockatoos, are less comfortable in captivity. Cockatoos and corellas require a lot of space and are easily bored, often becoming destructive if they are not kept entertained. People who keep parrots as pets often find that the parrot forms a close bond with one family member and dislikes the others. This is probably related to the fact that parrots pair-bond in the wild, so they are simply mimicking wild behaviour in a human setting. A less natural

Above, clockwise from top left: A corella paces along a windowsill. Cockatoo species can cause damage to wooden houses by tearing at sills and door frames with their beaks; Wildlife sanctuaries usually allow a chance to interact with the more common species; Rainbow Lorikeets take a plunge in an artificial bath; Flocking on telephone lines.

result of parrots being held in captivity is their ability to copy human voices. Parrots are excellent mimics and are renowned for being able to "speak" in captivity. Mysteriously, they don't practise mimicry in the wild, and this behaviour is seen only in caged parrots. Parrots are intelligent birds and probably try to mimic humans because of the affectionate "pair bond" that is formed between a parrot and its keeper.

Cockatoos

Family: *Cacatuidae*

Cockatoos are not unique to Australia. New Guinea, the Philippines and Indonesia also have cockatoos, but they remain more abundant on this continent, with fourteen native species, than anywhere else in the world. A feature that sets cockatoos apart from other parrots is the movable crest. Although generally not as brightly plumed as other parrots, cockatoos reserve much of their colour for this perky tuft, which varies in size and colour from species to species and is raised or lowered as a form of communication. The smallest cockatoo, the Cockatiel, has a brilliantly plumed, pale yellow crest. The largest species is the Palm Cockatoo, which occupies tropical northern rainforest and woodlands on Cape York Peninsula. Most other cockatoos are considered birds of the forests and woodlands. Only three cockatoo species, the Galah, Gang-Gang and Major Mitchell's Cockatoo, have plumage that almost rivals the Psittacidae parrots, with hues of pink, grey and rosy red. Most other species can loosely be considered either a black or white species. Black-Cockatoos consist of five species in the genus *Calyptorhynchus*, which translates as "hidden beak" — a reference to the habit of some species of fluffing up their cheek feathers to cover part of the beak. All have mostly black plumage that differs between the sexes of each species to include either cheek patches, coloured undertail coverts or body speckling. White cockatoos include the Sulphur-crested Cockatoo and three corella species, all of which are similarly attired in white plumage with blushes of colour on the face, or crest, and underwing and undertail coverts.

Cockatoos enjoy remarkable longevity. Captive birds can live for more than 50 years, but even in the wild some have a similar lifespan to humans. The oldest recorded cockatoo was a Little Corella that was tagged in 1901. It was found dead on the roadside in 1972 — making it 71 years old.

Top: Pretty in pink — Major Mitchell's Cockatoo is one of the most vibrant species. **Right:** The Gang-gang Cockatoo is unique in being the only cockatoo to have a wholly red "feather-duster" type crest.

Sulphur-crested Cockatoo *Cacatua galerita*

Australia's best known cockatoo is undoubtedly the large, white and yellow Sulphur-crested Cockatoo, with its cheeky demeanour and raucous shriek. This widespread species forms huge flocks and becomes very attached to regular, communal roost sites, rarely abandoning them, even if it means flying tens of kilometres to feeding grounds.

FEATURES: Males and females look alike, with white bodies, large yellow crests and a yellowish tinge over the ear coverts. In flight, the underside of the tail and wings flash yellow. In the north-west, the race *fitzroyi* is smaller with a bluish ring around the eye and less (or no) colour on the ears. Juveniles have a pale brown, rather than black, iris.

DIET & HABITAT: These birds live in a diverse range of habitats, including eucalypt woodlands, open woodlands, agricultural lands (particularly wheat and grain fields), suburban areas and rainforest. One of the more omnivorous species, they eat nuts, fruit, insects and larvae, grass seeds and the roots of some plants. This opportunistic diet has led to their widespread range.

BEHAVIOUR: Many people encounter these extroverted birds as pets that are known for their mimicry and piercing shouts of "Scratch Cocky!" In the wild, they are just as sociable, forming large, noisy flocks that post a sentry to warn other members of danger. Sulphur-crested Cockatoos are intelligent birds (their cognitive skills have been likened to that of a four-year-old child). When bored, they can become destructive and may use their beaks to defoliate trees or destroy wooden houses.

BREEDING: The male's crest is a courtship adornment that he raises and lowers while head bobbing. Pairs breed from May–Sept in the north and Aug–Jan in the south, laying 2–4 eggs in a hollow tree limb, tree trunk, or hole in a cliff. Males and females incubate the eggs for around 30 days. At 6–8 weeks of age, chicks depart the nest.

PREDATORS & THREATS: Clearing of large, old trees threatens ability to nest. Goannas may eat eggs and Dingoes and foxes may prey on feeding birds.

Above: Sulphur-crested Cockatoos form noisy permanent roosts.

DIET: Nuts, seeds, fruit, insects and larvae, roots

HABITAT: Wet eucalypt forests to mangroves and semi-arid and suburban areas

LENGTH: 45–50 cm

VOICE: Raucous screeches and grinding noises

STATUS: Common to abundant

Above, clockwise from top left: Feeding; When at rest, one foot is drawn up to the body; With the crest erect; Preening the feathers.

Named after Sir Thomas Mitchell, the explorer who wrote about this bird in 1835, this cockatoo is probably Australia's most magnificently coloured Cacatua *species. It is also one of the few parrots that vigorously defends a permanent breeding territory of several kilometres.*

FEATURES: The glorious colours of this bird include salmon pink underwing and undertail coverts and a spectacular white-tipped crest with a red base striped through with gold in the *leadbeateri* race. There are two races. The central and northern *mollis* has no yellow in the crest. Female *leadbeateri* Major Mitchell's have red eyes and a wider yellow crest band.

DIET & HABITAT: Preferred habitats are lightly timbered grasslands, agricultural lands, Mulga, mallee, open scrublands and pine woodlands, as well as well-watered areas of the inland. Major Mitchell's Cockatoos forage largely on the ground on grass seeds, grains, tubers and seeds of annual plants, as well as insect larvae.

BEHAVIOUR: These birds are more wary and less gregarious than most cockatoo species. They rarely form large flocks, preferring small groups of around twelve birds. Like other cockatoos, they may spend many hours deliberately stripping leaves from trees, probably to keep their beaks sharp.

BREEDING: Major Mitchell's Cockatoos need a large breeding territory of many kilometres and will chase away intruding birds. In the north, pairs breed from May–Sept; in the south, from Aug–Dec. One to four eggs are laid in a hollow and both male and female incubate them (often females by night and males by day) for around 30 days. Chicks fledge at 7–8 weeks and are independent sixteen weeks later.

PREDATORS & THREATS: Numbers of these birds have declined since European occupation, probably due to clearing of suitable nest trees and illegal smuggling of eggs.

Above: *Leadbeateri* subspecies have red and yellow crests.

DIET: Seeds, grains, tubers, insect larvae

HABITAT: Sparsely timbered woodlands, scrublands, riverine woodlands

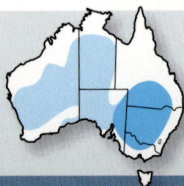

LENGTH: 35–40 cm

VOICE: Wavering, undulating screech of "ar-ai-ar-a-ar-iagh"

STATUS: Uncommon but Secure

Above: With the crest lowered, these birds are less flamboyant, but still blush-pink.

One of Australia's most common and playful cockatoo species, the seemingly inane Galah, has garnered such a reputation as an avian twit that its name has become a slang term. Its antics are probably so well-renowned because it is one of the most widespread and common cockatoo species. The name Galah is taken from an Aboriginal name for this bird.

FEATURES: The Galah's crest is not colourful, but it makes up for it with its pale grey and pink body feathers. There are three recognised subspecies. Race *roseicapilla* has red lores around the eye, rather than grey or white for *assimilis* race. *Albiceps* race inhabits south-eastern areas. Females have pink eyes while males have dark brown eyes.

DIET & HABITAT: Galahs thrive almost anywhere they can forage for seeds in open woodlands or grasslands near tall nest trees and water. Seed-bearing plants and grasses comprise most of their diet. They are often seen feeding on road verges in wheatbelt areas.

BEHAVIOUR: Galahs inhabit semi-arid areas where infrequent rain induces the larrikin behaviour for which these birds are known. This includes hanging upside down, pirouetting, and flapping around in puddles in an effort to clean feathers and perhaps deter lice. Galahs have also been seen flying into willy-willies, seemingly for pure sport. They roost communally and feed in flocks, walking, when on the ground, with a typical side-to-side swagger.

BREEDING: Galahs mate for life using the same nest hollow for many years. A distinctive nesting trait is lining the nest with gum leaves. Males also chew away a patch of bark around the nest's entrance, maybe to mark territory or deter goannas. Breeding season varies from north to south. Both sexes incubate the 3–4 eggs for 28–30 days.

PREDATORS & THREATS: Galahs are a favourite food for larger birds of prey such as Peregrine Falcons.

Above: Galahs prefer sparsely timbered habitat.
Right, top to bottom: When landing, the Galah's colours are even more apparent; A typical nest location in a branch cavity.

DIET: Seeds and grasses
HABITAT: Diverse; open woodlands and grasslands, semi-arid areas

LENGTH: 35–38 cm
VOICE: Metallic, sharp "chzink-chzink"
STATUS: Common and abundant

Naturalists from Cook's Endeavour *voyage first recorded this endemic species near Cooktown in 1770, where artist Sydney Parkinson sketched it and created the first European illustration of an Australian bird. It is the country's most common black-cockatoo species and occurs in all mainland States.*

FEATURES: Most taxonomists recognise five subspecies of Red-tailed Black-Cockatoo, varying in colour, size, habitat and beak size. Across all races, male and female plumage differs. Males have black, tapered crests and a crimson band on the outer tail feathers. Females and juveniles are spotted with yellow over the entire body, except for the wing-tips, with yellow undertail coverts.

DIET & HABITAT: Habitat ranges from coastal woodlands and forests to arid Mulga and casuarina scrublands, mallee country and timbered agricultural areas. Usually they reside close to water. Seeds of she-oaks, bloodwoods and other eucalypts are favoured, but these birds also eat seeds of banksias and hakeas. They feed mostly in the trees, but sometimes forage on the ground after wildfires, when some plant species drop their opened seedpods.

BEHAVIOUR: These cockatoos are nomadic and flocks can be huge, containing around 100 birds following the seeding of their favourite foods. Noisy flocks descend to drink at morning and evening. Aborigines from Western Australia's Pallinup River named this bird *Carrer,* in reference to a common loud vocalisation of this species.

BREEDING: Breeding season depends on location and subspecies. Although uncommon, some have been recorded brooding twice a year. Nest hollows are usually very high up in tree trunks and are used for many years. Black-cockatoos enter the hollow tail-first, and tear away bark at the entrance to add to the lining. Only one egg is laid, very seldom two, and the female incubates it for about 30 days.

PREDATORS & THREATS: The single eggs are vulnerable to predation.

Right: Males are larger and have red on the tail. **Opposite, clockwise from top left:** A female stretches her wings, showing underwing colour; Female eating; Females have smaller crests.

DIET: Seeds and grasses
HABITAT: Diverse; woodlands and grasslands from coastal to semi-arid areas
LENGTH: 50–65 cm

VOICE: Sometimes squeaky; often a grating, metallic "karraak" or "carrer"
STATUS: Threatened in the south-east; Secure elsewhere

This species is also known as Baudin's Black-Cockatoo after the French navigator who brought it to the attention of the scientific community. It differs only slightly in appearance from the similar Short-billed Black-Cockatoo due to its longer beak. Both species have white tail bands and cheek patches.

FEATURES: Almost identical to the Short-billed Black-Cockatoo but for the extended upper mandible, voice and behaviour. Females have grey rings around the eyes while males have red lores. Both sexes have long, white-panelled tails and uniform black upper- and underwing colour. Juveniles look similar to females.

DIET & HABITAT: This species is confined to woodlands and temperate eucalypt forests in the continent's far south-west. Wood-boring larvae add to a diet that is otherwise largely comprised of seeds, particularly the seeds of Karri gums, Marri, hakea and banksia. However, they also eat the flowers of the Marri gum and search for insect larvae beneath bark, as well as consuming orchard fruit, such as apples and pears.

BEHAVIOUR: Large flocks of up to 1000 birds may form during the colder months but mostly they are seen in pairs or small groups. Long-billed Black-cockatoos are locally nomadic, moving only short distances to find food.

BREEDING: Usually, Long-billed Black-Cockatoos nest very high in dense forests of tall Karri or Marri eucalypts, lining the nest with woodchips. Two eggs are laid in each clutch and the female incubates them for 3–4 weeks. Only one egg will usually hatch. Chicks fledge at 10–11 weeks of age and remain with the family group even after they mature.

PREDATORS & THREATS: Logging of old-growth forests severely limits suitable nest sites.

Above: A male Long-billed Black-Cockatoo alights on a banksia flower. Males are distinguished by the red lores around the eye and a charcoal-black beak. Females have a grey eye ring and a paler bill.

DIET: Seeds of Karri, Marri, hakea, banksia; wood-boring larvae and insects

HABITAT: Woodlands and temperate gum forests

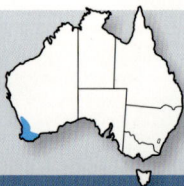

LENGTH: 55–60 cm

VOICE: A clear, whistling "wieer-ier" or "whyie-rrk"

STATUS: Endangered

This species was once thought to be a white-tailed species of the Yellow-tailed Black-Cockatoo, and later of the Long-billed Black-Cockatoo; however, studies have shown it to be a species in its own right. Some people refer to this bird as Carnaby's Cockatoo, as naturalist I.C. Carnaby was the first to notice that the shorter beak of this species distinguished it from other similar-looking cockatoos.

FEATURES: Superficially very similar to the Long-billed Black-Cockatoo and Yellow-tailed Black-Cockatoo, but for its smaller size, white cheek patches and shorter bill.

DIET & HABITAT: Occupies woodlands, farmlands, mallee country, pine forests and sandplains, where its usual feeding method is foraging on the ground or in the trees for seeds of hakeas, banksias, dryandras and some eucalypts. During winter, or when food is short, this species will become nomadic and move to coastal heath and other woodlands in search of food. It has also been known to visit pine plantations and feast on pine nuts.

BEHAVIOUR: Like the Long-billed Black-Cockatoo, this species is usually seen in pairs or small groups, except for in winter when it may seek the shelter of larger flocks.

BREEDING: Breeding occurs from Aug–Nov, with nests often constructed in hollows in Wandoo or Salmon Gums. Females shave off woodchips from the inside of the hollow to line the deep nest. Two eggs are laid and the female sits on them for around 30 days. When the chicks hatch, both parents feed them, and they leave the nest at around eleven weeks of age.

PREDATORS & THREATS: Deforestation for agricultural purposes has limited this species' natural food source in some areas, probably forcing brooding females off the nest to find food, thus affecting hatching.

Above: Short-billed Black-Cockatoos, like all cockatoos, nest in tree hollows but spend the night roosting in trees, unless incubating eggs.

DIET: Seeds of hakeas, banksias, dryandras, eucalypts and pines
HABITAT: Woodlands, farmlands, mallee, sandplains

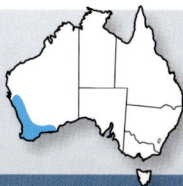

LENGTH: 55–60 cm
VOICE: A high, wavering "wy-ieee-la" or "aa-ieer-la"
STATUS: Endangered

*Most people recognise three races of this species — **lathami**, **erebus** and **halmaturinus**. Despite its common name, this species is, in fact, no more glossy than any other black-cockatoo and the misnomer, coupled with the male's superficial resemblance to the Red-tailed Black-Cockatoo, often sees bird-watching novices misidentify this bird.*

FEATURES: Males have a red panel on the tail, while the female's undertail feathers are pale red, fringed with orange. Females have irregular yellow feathering on the face and neck, where males have only a few random spots and slightly lighter feathering on the crown and neck. A defining characteristic in comparison to the Red-tailed Black-Cockatoo is that the Glossy Black-Cockatoo is smaller and has a larger bill relative to its body size. Both males and females also have smaller crests, which they rarely raise.

DIET & HABITAT: Exists almost entirely on the seeds of she-oaks (casuarinas), which subsequently reduces this species' habitats to those that have a good supply of these trees. Although reliant on she-oak seeds, Glossy Black-Cockatoos sometimes also eat the seeds of angophoras, wattles and eucalypts and may take insect larvae.

BEHAVIOUR: Glossy Black-Cockatoos rarely fly in large flocks, instead forming small groups of around ten individuals.

Most feeding occurs in the treetops and they rarely come to ground except to drink. On the ground, their short legs make walking awkward. Glossy Black-Cockatoos are tolerant of humans and may become tame in parks and gardens. Vocalisations are a wheezy "kee-airrk" or "airr-riiek" and are less screechy than those of most cockatoos.

BREEDING: A single egg is laid from Mar–Aug in a woodchip-lined hollow high in a dead tree. Incubation takes about 29 days, over which time the male brings food. The hatchling remains in the nest for 9–10 weeks.

PREDATORS & THREATS: Glossy Black-Cockatoos have declined across their former range. Clearing of casuarinas is an ongoing threat.

Above: A male chews on a juicy green shoot.
Right, top to bottom: Females of this species have a ruff-like patch of yellow feathers on the neck; The male's red tail panel on display.

DIET: Seeds, especially of casuarinas, wattles, eucalypts, angophoras
HABITAT: Forests, woodlands with plenty of she-oaks

LENGTH: 46–50 cm
VOICE: Wheezy, grating "airr-riiek", "kee-aiirk" or "aireek"
STATUS: Secure within limited habitat

Yellow-tailed Black-Cockatoo *Calyptorhynchus funereus*

This distinctive species is difficult to confuse with any of Australia's other cockatoos. Most ornithologists recognise two races, funereus *and* xanthanotus, *although a third race,* whitei, *possibly exists in western Victoria and south-east South Australia. Populations of this species on the Eyre Peninsula in South Australia are considered critically endangered.*

FEATURES: Males and females are similar but can be differentiated by the yellow cheek patch (larger in females) and skin around the eyes, (red in males and light grey in females). Both sexes have long tails with yellow panels. Juveniles look like females but juvenile males have a smaller cheek patch.

DIET & HABITAT: A range of habitats are used by this species; however, it seems to favour pine plantations and densely timbered wet sclerophyll forests.

Above: Females and males alike have bright yellow tail panels.

Yellow-tailed Black-Cockatoos forage, usually in flocks, for pine cones and the seeds of native trees and ground plants. Like most cockatoo species, they will also eat insect larvae on occasion, particularly wood-borers found under pine bark.

BEHAVIOUR: Despite sometimes forming flocks of up to 200 individuals, Yellow-tailed Black-Cockatoos are mostly seen in pairs or small family groups of fewer than twenty birds. When foraging, flocks may separate but remain in vocal contact. In the air, these large birds have an erratic flight, beating their wings rather slowly for such a large species.

BREEDING: Breeding season differs depending on the birds' range; in the north from Mar–Aug, with southern birds breeding Oct–Apr. A hollow is found high in a large tree and both parents help line it with woodchips. Two eggs are laid and incubated for about 28 days; however, only one chick usually survives. Chicks leave the nest at about eleven weeks of age.

PREDATORS & THREATS: This species has declined in some areas. Deforestation, predation of eggs by the Common Brushtail Possum and bees swarming in tree hollows, as well as increased predation of hatchlings by birds of prey in cleared areas, may be responsible for the decrease in populations.

DIET: Seeds and nuts, including pine nuts; insects such as wood-borers

HABITATS: Wet sclerophyll forests; pine plantations

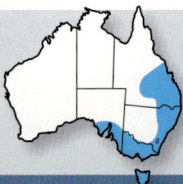

LENGTH: 58–65 cm

VOICE: Loud, penetrating "why-eela" that carries over a distance

STATUS: Secure; Endangered on Eyre Peninsula

Above: A more solid cheek patch and light grey lores around the eyes set the female apart from the male.

Western Corellas are similar to Long-billed Corellas, except that they occupy a more south-westerly range, with two subspecies butleri *(regarded as* derbyi *by some ornithologists) and* pastinator.

FEATURES: Like all corellas, Western Corellas are largely white with a pale yellow wash under the wings and rosy colouration on the face. The bill is slightly longer than the Little Corella's and shorter than the Long-billed Corella's, while the crest is longer than those of other species, although still wholly white. The eye rings are blue-grey with crimson-pink lores extending from the beak to the eye.

DIET & HABITAT: These birds shelter and forage near timbered agricultural lands or in densely wooded forests and woodlands. Large flocks feed mostly on the ground, using their beaks to dig through the soil in search of roots and corms. This activity can lend the plumage a redder colour from the soil.

BEHAVIOUR: Corellas are known to sift through the soil of freshly planted wheat fields — a trait that has not endeared them to farmers. Noisy, large flocks form and fly daily to water.

BREEDING: Corellas become very attached to their regular nesting sites and use the same tree hollow for many years. In the north of the range, Wandoo and Salmon Gum are popular nesting trees. In the south, Jarrah or Marri are preferred. Nesting takes place from Aug–Dec, with the female laying 1–3 eggs that both parents incubate for 24–29 days. Chicks hatch with a covering of soft yellowish down and leave the nest at about seven weeks of age, although they remain dependent on their parents for a further four weeks.

PREDATORS & THREATS: Populations of Western Corellas have declined over the past 200 years, the birds shot dead because of a perception that they were agricultural pests, but numbers are now growing again. Deforestation is a threat to this species, which has a very small range in South-West Western Australia.

Above: The beak is less finely pointed than that of the Long-billed Corella, and the crest is markedly longer.

DIET: Mostly roots, corms and seeds; fond of wheat

HABITAT: Woodlands and forests

LENGTH: 36–39 cm

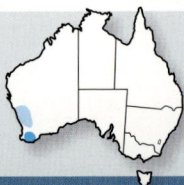

VOICE: A nasal, resonant "aier-ek, aier-rr-k", screeches and guttural croaks

STATUS: Vulnerable

Above, top to bottom: Pairs are monogamous and
mutually preen; A roost tree.

Little Corella *Cacatua sanguinea*

The common name of this species is misleading — the Western Corella grows to a similar size and the Long-billed Corella usually grows just a few centimetres larger. However, one characteristic is noticeably smaller on this species — the crest. Little Corellas are probably the birds that navigator William Dampier mentioned in his journal in 1699, when he described a "Sort of white Parrots, which flew a great many together".

FEATURES: The four subspecies—*normantoni*, *sanguinea*, *gymnopis* and *westralensis* — differ only slightly. Superficially, these birds seem similar to the Western Corella, but have less pink colouration around the eyes and beak (particularly for the race *sanguinea)*, and no pink on the chin or throat. Beneath the eye, the blue-grey eye-ring is baggy and more prominent. Brighter yellow underwing coverts also differentiate this corella from others.

DIET & HABITAT: Little Corellas enjoy a riverine existence and often roost in trees near watercourses or on nearby timbered plains. Mulga, mallee and savanna woodlands are also suitable environments. Roots, corms and seeds are the mainstays of their diet, although they sometimes excavate and eat insect larvae and eat some flowers in the trees. Little Corellas found near suburban areas are probably escaped aviary birds, rather than wild individuals.

BEHAVIOUR: A cacophony of squawks often heralds the arrival of a flock of corellas, sometimes numbering as many as 70,000 individuals. Like most cockatoos, they are very vocal, whether in flight or at roost. Their habits can be quite destructive, with large flocks known to rapidly defoliate trees.

BREEDING: Eggs are laid in Aug–Jan in the south of the range and Jul–Nov in the north. Rain also affects egg-laying in arid areas. Favoured nest sites are in trees that line waterholes, as well as in mangrove forests, termite mounds and cliffs in the north. Both sexes incubate the 2–4 eggs for around 24 days.

PREDATORS & THREATS: Corellas may be preyed upon by large raptor species. Deforestation can also be a threat.

Above: On the wing. **Right, top to bottom**: A breeding pair; Roost trees are reused continually.

DIET: Seeds, corms, bulbs
HABITAT: Timbered riverine and savanna woodlands, Mulga, mallee

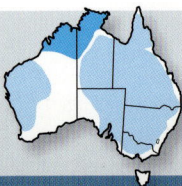

LENGTH: 36–39 cm
VOICE: Guttural to piercing "aier-ek, aier-rr-k"
STATUS: Secure

Since European occupation of the continent, Long-billed Corella populations have fluctuated. While their range has decreased considerably, populations are increasing and are now considered secure.

FEATURES: The crest of this species is rarely raised and is somewhat shorter than that of the other two corella species. Red–pink facial colouring is usually more pronounced, especially on the throat. The distinctive bill has an obvious elongated, sharp-tipped upper mandible (jaw). Feathers under the wings and tail are yellow.

DIET & HABITAT: Woodlands near waterways are the most common haunts of Long-billed Corellas, especially where there are large River Red Gums to roost in and nearby grasslands where these birds forage for grass-seeds, grains, roots, bulbs and corms. A favourite is the corm of Onion Grass (*Romulia longifolia*).

BEHAVIOUR: Gregarious flocks roost at night and visit watering holes around dusk and dawn daily, except during the breeding season when they are mostly seen in pairs. If disturbed, Long-billed Corellas emit a loud, harsh, screeching sound.

BREEDING: The breeding season is dependent on rainfall in arid areas, but most egg-laying occurs from Jul–Dec in a Manna Gum, Sugar Gum or River Red Gum. Hollows are used for many years, but this bird's habit of stripping away chips of inner bark to line the nest often destroys the site over time. Usually 2–4 eggs are laid and are incubated by both sexes for about 25 days.

PREDATORS & THREATS: These Corellas face a lack of suitable nesting hollows, interference with eggs and attack by large birds of prey, as well as deforestation.

Above: The long, dagger-like bill helps them shovel up bulbs. **Right, clockwise from top left:** Some have particularly fuchsia facial colours; Leaving a nesting hollow; Pairs probably bond for life; Huge flocks can gather on agricultural lands; Showing the pale yellow wash on the underwings.

DIET: Grass-seeds, roots, grains, bulbs and corms
HABITAT: Riverine woodlands with adjacent grasslands

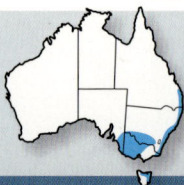

LENGTH: 38–41 cm
VOICE: Thrice repeated falsetto "ar-aer-ek, ar-aer-ek"
STATUS: Secure

Male Gang-gang Cockatoos are difficult to confuse with any other species due to their brilliant red heads and small, feathery crests — even the duller-coloured females are distinguished by this characteristic wispy plume. They are especially conspicuous around Canberra and are the faunal emblem of the ACT.

FEATURES: Males are the more colourful, with crimson-tufted heads compared to the female's drab grey face and crest. Most of the female's colour is on her barred underwings and buff-grey to orange-red breast feathers. Both sexes are entirely grey on the upper surface, with long wings and a short, square tail. Juveniles look like females, but males have red and grey speckling on the face and breast.

DIET & HABITAT: Gang-gangs are well adapted to life in cool climates. They are common in the highlands and eucalypt forests of the Blue Mountains, Australian Alps and Snowy Mountains, moving to lower altitudes during winter. Fruit, seeds, nuts and berries, particularly of the hawthorn and Roman Cypress, comprise most of their diet so they seldom forage on the ground.

BEHAVIOUR: These capable fliers are mostly seen in pairs or small groups, except in winter when they form larger flocks. When feeding, vocalisations are like the squeaking of a rusty gate. In the air, their "er-eck" sounds like the prolonged squeak of a cork being drawn from a wine bottle. Gang-gang Cockatoos are not wary birds and can become quite tame.

BREEDING: Gang-gangs prefer an almost vertical, high tree hollow up to 27 m above the ground. Breeding occurs from Oct–Jan, extending to Aug–Mar. Woodchips create a nest-lining for the 2–3 eggs, which are incubated by the female at night and the male by day for 25–30 days.

PREDATORS & THREATS: Gang-gangs are vulnerable in New South Wales. Clearing of habitat and hollow trees threatens breeding. Psittacine cirovirus disease also affects this species.

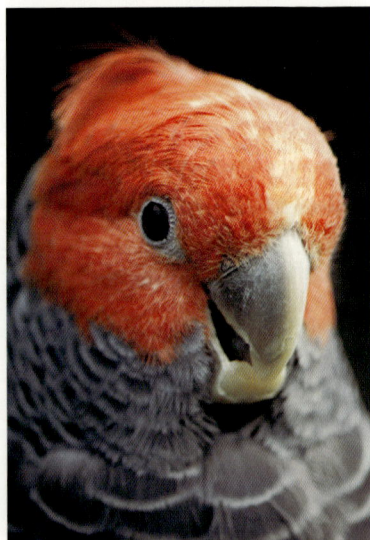

Above: Males have scalloped grey on the body with a crimson-tufted head.

DIET: Arboreal eaters of seeds, nuts, berries, fruit

HABITAT: Highland woodlands and eucalypt forests

LENGTH: 33–36 cm

VOICE: Prolonged creaky "gr-raer-ir-iek"

STATUS: Vulnerable in NSW; Secure elsewhere

Above, top to bottom: Both sexes sharpen the beak by gnawing; Grasping claws help a female clutch at seeds and stems.

The Cockatiel is the smallest, most graceful of the Australian cockatoos and is the sole member of the genus Nymphicus. *Like the Budgerigar, this is one of Australia's best-known endemic parrots because it has been widely adopted as an aviary bird.*

FEATURES: Cockatiels have a large yellow crest (relative to body size) and body plumage of graduating grey, with yellow, white, and rosy-red cheeks. In captivity, breeding has created plumage variations, but colour and patterning are more uniform in the wild. Females have less bright yellow on the face and lack the male's white outer cheek markings. Females are also a paler silver-grey, except for the shoulders and outer wing tips, and have a barred yellow and grey tail, whereas the male's is simply pale grey.

DIET & HABITAT: Cockatiels seek sparsely timbered, open woodlands close to a water supply. Feeding occurs quietly on the ground, where they blend in well while eating acacia and grass seeds.

BEHAVIOUR: Less noisy than larger cockatoo species, the Cockatiel is also known as the Quarrion because of the sound of its call. The birds are nomadic and move to coastal areas during drought. They may also migrate south in summer and north in winter. Large flocks form, but Cockatiels are often seen in pairs when breeding.

BREEDING: Part of this bird's aviary appeal is that it breeds well in captivity. Wild Cockatiels breed from Aug–Sep in the south and Apr–Aug in the north, in hollows in dead trees or tree stumps. Both sexes incubate a clutch of 4–6 eggs for 21–23 days. Chicks do not leave the nest for about five weeks.

PREDATORS & THREATS: Cockatiels are prey for large raptor species. Their low nest sites (at only 1–10 m above ground) make chicks vulnerable.

Above: Females usually have less yellow and white on the face than males, and more grey.

DIET: Seeds of grasses and acacias

HABITAT: Diverse, including coastal, arid and semi-arid grasslands and woodlands

LENGTH: 31–33 cm

VOICE: Slightly husky, shrill "whee-it", "quarr-i" or "querr-eel"

STATUS: Secure

Above: Males generally have a ring of white behind the red-orange ear coverts and brighter yellow on the face and crest.

The continent's largest cockatoo species is sometimes referred to as the Goliath Cockatoo because of its size. The species was only recognised in Australia in 1848, although a drawing was made of a specimen in the islands north of Australia in 1764. Palm Cockatoos are also found in New Guinea and the Aru Islands.

FEATURES: The tapered black crest of this species, coupled with its size, large down-curved bill and red, featherless cheek patch make it highly distinctive. Of all Australia's black-cockatoos, it alone has no colour banding on the tail. Males and females appear very similar, although the female's bill and cheek patch are slightly smaller.

DIET & HABITAT: This rainforest species has a small distribution in rainforest at the tip of Cape York Peninsula and rarely ventures into other habitats beyond the woodlands or eucalypt forests at the rainforest's fringe. They exist mostly on fruit, berries, nuts and seeds but will also eat leaf buds and some insect larvae. Their large, powerfully curved beaks enable them to crack open the hard shells of pandanus fruit, which are a particular favourite.

BEHAVIOUR: Palm Cockatoos are usually seen in pairs or singly, with larger groups occasionally gathering to display or move to shared feeding grounds. At night, roosts are shared in tall, conspicuous dead trees. When excited, the naked red-orange cheek patch becomes a darker crimson.

BREEDING: Nests are made in hollows within vertical, broken-off tree branches in eucalypts on the forest's fringe, and are lined with a layer of twigs. From Aug–Feb the female lays a single, slightly oval egg and incubates it for around 35 days. After hatching, the chick spends 3–4 months in the hollow.

PREDATORS & THREATS: Destruction of habitat and nest hollows, largely through fire, is a major concern.

Above: The back-combed crest, bulky body and enormous, powerful jaws make this bird readily identifiable.

DIET: Nuts, seeds, fruit, berries, pandanus

HABITAT: Rainforest and fringing eucalypt forest

LENGTH: 55–65 cm

VOICE: A dual note rising in pitch to a piercing "aar-rraiik"

STATUS: Secure within a very limited range

Above: At rest, the crest is lowered, but the head still appears large on the short body.

Parrots

Family: *Psittacidae*

Parrots in the Psittacidae family are commonly referred to as the "typical" parrots — although their wide distribution and range of fabulously varied colours make them anything but typical. For the purpose of discussing Australian species, the family can be divided into two basic subfamilies — the Psittacinae (parrots, parakeets and fig-parrots all separated into distinct genera) and the Loriinae (lorikeets). Like all other Psittaciformes, they have zygodactylous toes, curved bills and powder-down feathers.

For the most part, the males are the more brightly attired of these parrots; however, the Eclectus Parrot is a notable exception. Colour variations probably evolved for two reasons: firstly to distinguish species with overlapping ranges, and secondly to make the birds either distinctive (to attract a mate) or camouflaged within their habitat. Red and yellow feather colours form from carotenes, the same pigments that colour carrots. Black feathers are the result of melatonin, which also colours human skin. Blue feathers appear blue due to Tindall scattering — when feathers reflect and absorb only some of the wavelengths in white light — the same effect that makes the sky appear blue. Along with a kaleidoscope of wonderful colours, some parrots also use fluorescence to help them attract a mate; studies show that certain feathers glow under ultraviolet (UV) light. These cryptic mating codes would not attract the attention of mammalian predators, which cannot see UV light.

Being smaller, swifter and more abundant than the larger cockatoos, parrots inhabit a greater diversity of vegetation types. Some ornithologists group species based on their habitats or relatives: six small species in the genus *Neophema* are called the "grass parrots", rosella species form a group, and so do the so-called "magnificent parrots" in the *Polytelis* genus. None of these groups diverge from the "typical parrot" characteristics as much as the lorikeets do.

Top: Lorikeets are nectarivorous birds — unlike most typical parrots, which are seed-eaters. **Right:** Long tail feathers are not ideal for nesting in hollows, as this Rosella's tail damage shows.

Australian King-Parrot *Alisterus scapularis*

Heralded by a vivid flash of scarlet and emerald, the King-Parrot is a frequent visitor to backyards along Australia's eastern coast. Two subspecies are recognised. Scapularis *is by far the most common, although the smaller subspecies,* minor, *has a few distinct populations along the central and northern coast of eastern Queensland.*

FEATURES: Males have striking scarlet body plumage with green wings and tail, which becomes a deep almost purplish-blue at the base. Females have a greenish-yellow body that becomes red below the chest. They retain the same colour wings and undertail coverts as the males. Both sexes have a pale turquoise stripe down the wing, although it is often more obvious on the male. Juveniles resemble females but have brown eyes.

DIET & HABITAT: Rainforests and wet sclerophyll forests, along with palm forests and some mountain and cloud forests are their usual abodes. King-Parrots eat fruit, seeds and some nectar and blossoms. They are known to favour the berries from the Brush Turpentine (*Rhodamnia rubescens*) and Blue Lilly pilly (*Syzygium oleosum*).

BEHAVIOUR: Sociable and gregarious, King-Parrots form small flocks, usually with a maximum of around twenty individuals. They are also commonly seen in pairs and are often attracted to backyard birdfeeders; however, they remain naturally wary of humans.

BREEDING: King-Parrots choose very high nesting hollows (often in tree trunks) with a long chamber down to the nest. A clutch of 4–6 eggs is incubated by the female for around twenty days, after which she continues to brood the chicks for a further few weeks. The offspring fledge and leave the nest at about five weeks of age.

PREDATORS & THREATS: Although this species is widespread and secure, individual birds are threatened by feral cat predation, goannas taking eggs, land clearing and fire.

Above: Roost trees, often pines, are shared.

DIET: Fruit, seeds, berries, nectar and some flowers

HABITAT: Wet sclerophyll forests, rainforests, palm and cloud forests

LENGTH: 42–44 cm

VOICE: Clear "k-wiek" in flight and a harsh "karrak" call if threatened

STATUS: Secure

Above, top to bottom: Females are difficult to spot in the foliage; Males are more conspicuous.

The smaller Red-winged Parrot bears similar colouration to the Australian King-Parrot, but on closer inspection it is more lime-green than viridian and lacks the red underbody of the King-Parrot. This entirely separate — although related — species occupies the continent's northern aridlands and parts of the centre.

FEATURES: Males and females look alike; both are green on the head and body with a patch of crimson on the inside outer wing. Distinction is possible because the male's back is black and his eyes are red-orange, whereas the female's eyes are brown. Most ornithologists recognise two subspecies — *erythropterus* and *coccineopterus* — with distributions separated by a hybrid zone.

DIET & HABITAT: Red-winged Parrots are rather versatile when it comes to habitat and appreciate arid acacia woodlands, rainforests, mallee woodlands, brigalow and even mangrove forests. Some tree cover is required as they seldom feed on the ground, preferring to pick off fruit, seeds, blossoms, insects and nectar in the treetops or in shrubs.

BEHAVIOUR: Red-winged Parrots typically have a wavering, slow-flapping flight style. Small flocks are formed, but they are mostly seen in pairs and are timid in the wild. In the treetops,

Red-winged Parrots can be rather acrobatic, grasping foliage in their beaks and claws and dangling from stems to get at food.

BREEDING: A clutch of 3–6 eggs is laid in a hollow within a gum tree, often close to a waterhole. Females incubate the eggs for twenty days, exiting the nest only to be fed by the male at the hollow's entrance. Both male and female feed the fledglings, which fly at around five weeks of age.

PREDATORS & THREATS: Feral cats and birds of prey feed on these birds if caught. Deforestation and land clearing threatens most bird species.

Above: Males can be differentiated from females by their red-orange irises.

DIET: Fruit, seeds, flowers, insects and nectar
HABITAT: Acacia woodlands, rainforests, mallee, brigalow, mangrove forests

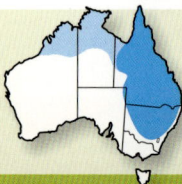

LENGTH: 31–32 cm
VOICE: Similar to a twittering Budgie from a distance; metallic "chrrrik-chrrrik"
STATUS: Secure

Above: Preening is a daily duty that "zips" feather barbs back into place, helps to prevent feather damage, and can strip away lice.

This species is made up of a number of subspecies that were previously classified as species in their own right, and as such have various common names that are well known and used locally. Thus the Port Lincoln Parrot (Barnardius zonarius zonarius), Twenty-eight Parrot (B. z. semitorquatus), Mallee Ringneck (B. z. barnardi) and Cloncurry Ringneck (B. z. macgillivrayi), although differing in voice and appearance, are all dealt with in this profile.

FEATURES: Appearance varies depending on race. All are green to yellow with blue on the cheeks and beneath the tail and wings. Colour saturation varies, with the Cloncurry Ringneck being the palest and the Port Lincoln Parrot the darkest. They are all characterised by the yellow "collar" that runs around the nape of the neck — giving the species its common name. Some races have a prominent red band at the base of the beak.

DIET & HABITAT: Combined, the four races cover most of the southern extent of the continent, from the semi-arid mallee, Mulga and spinifex of the Port Lincoln Parrot to the dense wet eucalypt forests favoured by the Twenty-Eight Parrot. Open forests and riverine woodlands suit the Cloncurry Ringneck. The Mallee Ringneck, as the name suggests, is a bird of the mallee and Mulga scrub and surrounding woodlands. Most races forage on the ground or in trees for seeds, gumnuts, gum blossoms, nectar, insect larvae, native fruit and some orchard fruit.

BEHAVIOUR: Human settlement has provided ringnecks with artificial water sources in dry habitats and with agricultural crops as a food source. By nature they are sociable and form small groups to large flocks in wheatbelt regions. When caged, these birds can be restless and aggressive.

BREEDING: Southern races breed later (Aug–Dec) than those in the north, which breed from Feb–Nov. A high tree hollow is chosen (when tall trees are available) and 4–6 eggs are incubated for 19–20 days. Males and females both feed fledglings, which vacate the nest at 5–6 weeks.

PREDATORS & THREATS: Habitat loss due to clearing (particularly of mallee country) is a problem. Feral cats, Dingoes, foxes and birds of prey will attack Australian Ringnecks when they are on the ground.

Right, clockwise from top left: The Twenty-eight Parrot got its name because its call is said to sound like "twen-ty-eight"; The Cloncurry Ringneck has the most limited distribution of all Australian Ringnecks; A Port Lincoln Parrot at the entrance to its nest hollow. In the Pilbara region of WA, a race of Port Lincoln Parrot, *occidentalis*, has no common name; Mallee Ringnecks have a red band around and above the cere, but are more turquoise-coloured on the face than other subspecies of Australian Ringneck.

DIET: Fruit, seeds and nuts
HABITAT: Diverse; from semi-arid to wet eucalypt forest — varies from subspecies to subspecies

LENGTH: 34–38 cm
VOICE: Varies for all subspecies from "klingit-klingit" to "twen-ty-eight"
STATUS: Secure

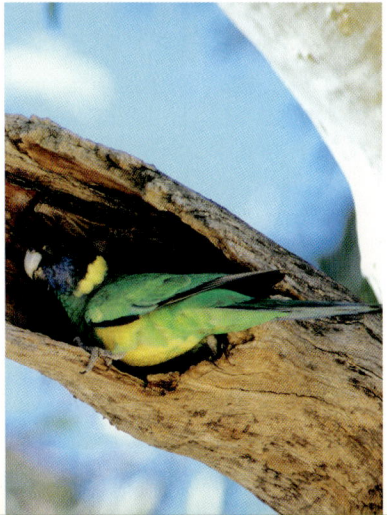

Double-eyed Fig-Parrots are Australia's smallest parrots, more closely resembling lovebirds than other native species. There are three confirmed races: macleayana, coxeni *and* marshalli. *The common name stems from an error made by early ornithologists, who, seeing a New Guinean race at a distance, mistook their facial markings for a twin set of eyes.*

FEATURES: All subspecies are lime–yellowish green with yellow banding under the wings. *Macleayana* is typified by a red forehead, leading to the name Red-browed Fig-Parrot. Males also have red below the eye. In contrast, the Blue-Browed Fig-Parrot (or Coxen's Fig-Parrot, *coxeni*) has blue above the beak and below the chin, with red-orange around the eye. Facial markings are less obvious on females. The *marshalli* female has no red on the face, while the male has mostly red with just a smear of blue above the eye.

DIET & HABITAT: An arboreal existence in the rainforest canopy suits these squat little parrots, which blend in well with the foliage and fruit. Fruit and nectar comprise most of their diet, with native figs being a special favourite.

BEHAVIOUR: When feeding, fig-parrots are quiet and well hidden, reserving their calls for when in flight. At night, they gather in communal roosts of up to 200 individuals.

BREEDING: Fig-Parrots gnaw out a tight-fitting hollow in the wood of a dead tree and lay a clutch of 2–3 eggs. Females incubate for eighteen days.

PREDATORS & THREATS: Cats, foxes, and clearing are threats. Coxen's Fig-Parrot is endangered in Qld and NSW.

Above: Males of *macleayana* race are the most colourful species, with red and blue on the face.

Above: Females of *macleayana* race are red above the ceres.

DIET: Fruit and berries, especially figs
HABITAT: Rainforest
LENGTH: 13–15 cm

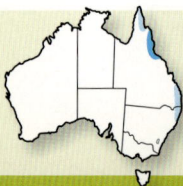

VOICE: Screeches when alarmed; "tseit-tseit-tseit" noise normal
STATUS: Two races are Secure; Coxen's is Endangered

Above: A male *C. d. macleayana* feeds a brooding female.

The Eclectus Parrot is one of the most fascinating parrot species because, for once, the female is brighter and more colourful than the male. So different are the colours of the male and female that they were regarded as two separate species for almost a century following their discovery in the Pacific in 1776. Australia's subspecies is macgillivrayi.

FEATURES: These parrots are strongly sexually dimorphic, with the scarlet and blue female impossible to mistake for the mostly green male. The female's beak is black; the male's upper beak is yellow-orange, and his lower beak is black. Males have flashes of scarlet on the flanks and a red iris. Females have yellow irises (although the eye appears black when the pupil is enlarged). It is thought that the male's colour helps him camouflage in the rainforest habitat while the female's brighter plumage may help her assert dominance in choosing a nest hollow and a mate — making her easy for males and other competing females to see.

DIET & HABITAT: Eclectus Parrots are a rainforest species, but will venture out to nearby woodlands and adjacent eucalypt forests when trees are fruiting. Their main diet is fruit, nuts and seeds.

BEHAVIOUR: Noisy flocks of up to 80 birds rest in roost trees. These birds will also fly across the sea — a subspecies from New Guinea forages for food on islands in the Torres Strait.

BREEDING: Unusually, Eclectus Parrots are believed to breed communally — with as many as eight birds (probably siblings) caring for offspring. Two eggs are laid in each clutch in tree hollows, often overhanging water. Eggs are incubated by the female for about 26 days.

PREDATORS & THREATS: Deforestation and predation by feral cats are threats.

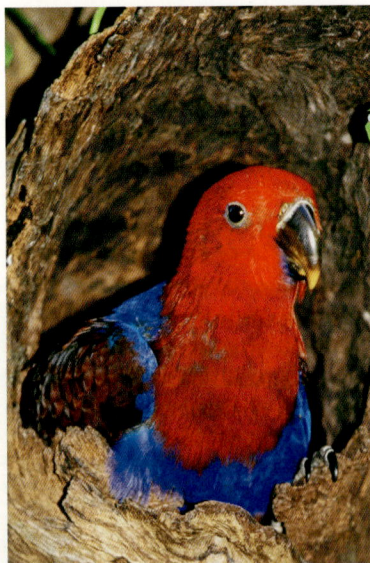

Above: A female in her nest hollow. **Opposite, clockwise from top left:** Females are crimson and blue; A male lets out a throaty "arrrk-arrrk-arrrk" screech; Eclectus parrots rarely come to ground, usually eating and roosting in treetops.

DIET: Fruit, seeds and nuts
HABITAT: Rainforest and adjacent woodlands and eucalypt forest

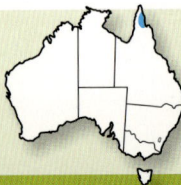

LENGTH: 40–43 cm
VOICE: Throaty and piercing "arrrrk-arrrk-arrrk" squawk
STATUS: Secure

A resident only of the rainforests of Cape York Peninsula and New Guinea, the Red-cheeked Parrot resembles the Eclectus Parrot in body shape and size, but not in colour. Despite vague similarities, it has no close Australian relatives and is the only member of the Geoffroyus genus on this continent. It was unknown to the scientific community in Australia until 1913, although Timorese specimens had come to attention in the early 19th century.

FEATURES: The male is the more colourful with a bright-red head and face and purple-blue crown. The body colour for both sexes is green. Juveniles have brown heads, which become green-brown for females and red for males at about two years of age. The underside of the body is leaf green, with a green-yellow undertail. The wings are dark blue-grey, becoming brilliant royal blue on the underwing coverts.

DIET & HABITAT: They live mostly in lowland tropical rainforest and surrounding woodlands and mangrove forests in a restricted area of Cape York. Seeds, nuts, berries and fruit are eaten high in the rainforest canopy, but it is thought they may take small invertebrates and plant matter as well.

BEHAVIOUR: Their habit of feeding noisily in the treetops, making a piercing "airk-airk-airk" or "honk-honk" sound, helps locate this otherwise well-camouflaged bird. Red-cheeked Parrots rarely come to the ground.

BREEDING: Like fig-parrots, this species uses its beak to actively carve out a hollow in the trunk or limb of a live eucalypt, rather than simply occupying an existing hole. Each clutch of 2–4 eggs is laid during the Aug–Dec breeding season and are incubated by the female, who is fed by the male while brooding. Offspring fledge and fly at about five weeks of age.

PREDATORS & THREATS: The island-like character of their habitat — rainforest surrounded by savannas — affords little resistance to threats.

Above: A female and juvenile at the entrance to the nesting hollow, which has been carved out in the stump of a vertical tree branch.

DIET: Nuts, seeds, berries and fruit, as well as some invertebrates

HABITAT: Small area of tropical rainforest

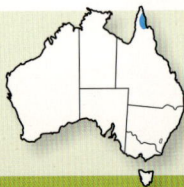

LENGTH: 21–24 cm

VOICE: Metallic "airk, airk, airk"

STATUS: Secure within a very restricted range

As its name implies, this parrot flies in large flocks that move rapidly across the sky. Although it is more closely related to the typical parrots than the lorikeets, it shares some habits with the latter group — a fact attributed to convergent evolution rather than any kind of shared ancestry.

FEATURES: Green and red plumage, coupled with this bird's swift, direct flight, lead some to mistake it for the King-Parrot. Distinctive differences are that the majority of its body is green, with scarlet at the base of the tail and under the wing coverts. The flight feathers are dark brown. Facial features are also very distinctive with a dark blue crown and red and yellow fringing the beak. Splashes of scarlet also adorn the outer shoulder and the tertial feathers.

DIET & HABITAT: Woodlands and forests with plenty of flowering vegetation are their favoured domains. Swift Parrots eat nectar and have rudimentary brush-like tongues; however, their tongues are in no way as specialised as those of the lorikeets. Tasmanian Blue Gums and Yellow Box are special favourites. Psyllid lerps (psyllid bug larvae encased in cocoons of sugary nectar) are also eaten.

BEHAVIOUR: Swift Parrots migrate south in spring and north to the mainland for winter. Researchers believe most migration occurs at night. On the mainland, they move nomadically to search for food. Swift Parrots fly and feed in small groups, and are frequently seen in the company of other honeyeaters in flowering trees.

BREEDING: Breeding and nesting occurs only in Tasmania and Bass Strait Islands from Sept–Dec. Several hollows may be located in one tree, each containing a clutch of 3–5 eggs laid on fine wood shavings. The female incubates the eggs for twenty days. Young leave the hollow at six weeks.

PREDATORS & THREATS: Numbers have been declining for some years; habitat destruction and predation by feral cats, birds and foxes are thought to have contributed.

Above: When preening, the scattered red-orange colouring on the underwings is apparent.

DIET: Nectar, pollen, psyllid lerps

HABITAT: Forest and woodlands with flowering plant species

LENGTH: 23–26 cm

VOICE: High musical notes of "chiwit, chiwit, chiwit"

STATUS: Endangered

The first written record of this bird's unusual name, which is of Aboriginal origin, was in 1830 when William Gardener referred to it as a "Budgerry Gann". Since then, this uniquely Australian bird —the only member of the Melopsittacus *genus —has become one of the best-known avian species around the globe. Its popularity as a pet means that it is kept in captivity throughout the world, where it is bred for its numerous colour variations and friendly, pleasant nature.*

FEATURES: Captive birds come in a range of colours, but both sexes of the wild bird are green and yellow with barred and scalloped feathers over the wings and head. The underside of the wing is a deep, vivid green — the prevailing colour when a flock of these birds is on the wing — with a pale yellow bar on the underwing and brown, blue-green edged wing tips. Juveniles are duller in colour.

DIET & HABITAT: The humble "Budgie" occupies most of the country with the exception of the far northern and southern extremities. Sparsely treed woodlands, grasslands, spinifex country, saltbush plains and riverine woodlands are all suitable environments for this versatile small parrot, which feeds largely on seeds, especially of Mitchell Grass and *Triodia* species.

BEHAVIOUR: In a good season, flocks of many thousands may form — wheeling across the sky with remarkable synchronicity — but most flocks number a few hundred. Budgerigars are nomadic, following the rains and seeding of grasses. Unusually for seed-eaters, they can forgo water for several days, but they are still usually found close to rivers or watercourses.

BREEDING: Nesting is often communal, with large flocks taking up hollows in a stand of large trees. They may breed several times in a good season, producing a clutch of 4–8 eggs each time. Incubation takes eighteen days. Offspring fledge at 4–5 weeks.

PREDATORS & THREATS: Large raptors such as the Black Falcon are predators.

Above: A typical nest hollow.

DIET: Seeds, especially Mitchell Grass and spinifex

HABITAT: Open grasslands and woodlands of the arid and semi-arid interior

LENGTH: 17–20 cm

VOICE: Melodius "tirrit, tir-rit, tirrit" or "tzzit-tzit-tzzit"

STATUS: Secure and abundant

Above, clockwise from top: Huge flocks form; Budgerigars are affectionate birds that preen and "feed" their partners; Mating occurs from June to January or anytime after rain.

Bourke's Parrot *Neopsephotus bourkii*

Explorer Major Thomas Mitchell first recorded this unusual, pastel-coloured parrot near the Bogan River in 1835, naming it bourkii *after Sir Richard Bourke, the then Governor of New South Wales. For some time, Bourke's Parrot was classified with the* Neophema *genus of grass parrots, but has since been reclassified in a genus of its own.*

FEATURES: It is markedly different to all other Australian species, with a pink and beige body, and wing feathers that are blue-violet (both on the upper and lower sides) and paler blue under the base of the tail. The central section of the upper wing is scalloped with brown and cream. Males also have a band of blue across the top of the cere. Females and juveniles are slightly paler in body colour than the males.

DIET & HABITAT: Arid and semi-arid grasslands, usually to the south of the Tropic of Capricorn, are the favoured domain of this desert-adapted bird. It is especially fond of Mulga habitat. The seeds of grasses and shrubs, as well as the shoots of some herbaceous plants, make up this parrot's diet.

BEHAVIOUR: Bourke's Parrot is a quiet, reclusive species that habitually flies in to drink at waterholes at dusk. It is rarely seen or heard, despite its relative abundance in the inland. Small flocks are formed and become nomadic when food is in short supply.

BREEDING: Breeding follows seasonal rainfall, often from Jul–Nov. Hollows are occupied in eucalypt or Desert Oak trees, and sometimes in smaller shrubs in sparsely vegetated areas. For 18–19 days, the female incubates a clutch of 3–6 eggs. At about four weeks the offspring fledge and leave the nest.

PREDATORS & THREATS: These ground-feeding birds are especially susceptible to attack from birds of prey, feral cats, Dingoes and foxes.

Left: A female preens her back feathers.

DIET: Seeds and shoots of herbs

HABITAT: Arid and semi-arid grasslands

LENGTH: 19–22 cm

VOICE: Melodius yet penetrating "chew-eet, chew-eet, chew-eet"

STATUS: Secure; populations are seasonally variant

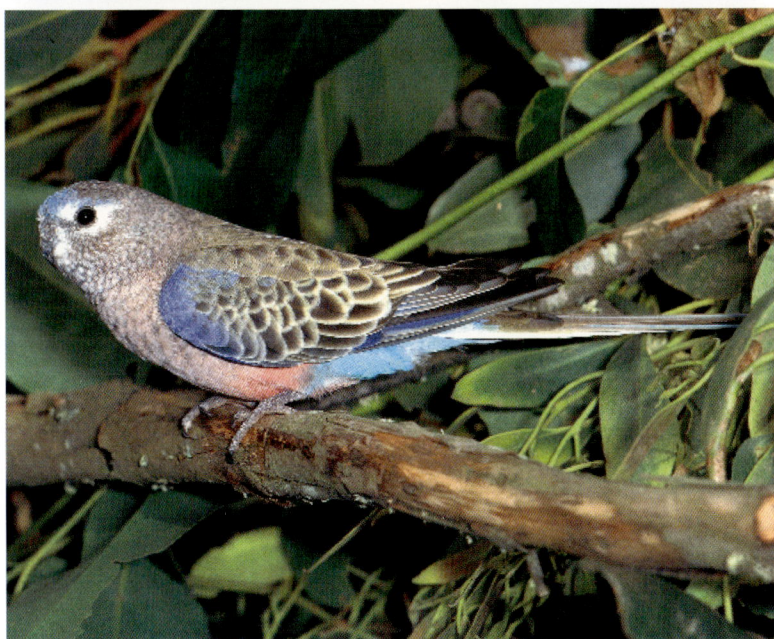

Above, top to bottom: The muted colours of both the female (top) and the male (bottom) blend in beautifully with the hues of soil and dry grasses.

Unfortunately, this species has the dubious distinction of being one of the world's rarest birds, with an estimated 150–400 individuals remaining in the wild. It is categorised as "Critically Endangered" on the IUCN Red List of Threatened Species, and conservation efforts continue in the hope of increasing populations.

FEATURES: Strangely, the orange belly feathers for which this species is named are not always very apparent, being on the lower belly and rather pale on females and juveniles. Elsewhere, its body superficially resembles other parrots in the *Neophema* genus, with an emerald green upper plumage, yellow underbelly graduating to pale green on the breast and chin, and blue on the wings' outer flight feathers. Juveniles lack the blue face band over the lores.

DIET & HABITAT: This species survives in just a small, mainly coastal area of sedgeland, salt marsh, fens and buttongrass in southern Victoria, South Australia and Tasmania. Seeds comprise most of the diet, including those of mainland salt-resistant species such as Shrubby Glasswort (*Sclerostegia arbuscula*) and Beaded Glasswort (*Sarcocornia quinqueflora*).

BEHAVIOUR: Orange-bellied Parrots are highly migratory, which may represent a threat to their limited population. When alarmed, they emit a quick, repetitive alarm call that sounds like a low, buzzing "zzt-zzt-zzt".

BREEDING: It was once thought that these birds bred in holes in the ground — an error made by naturalist John Gould, who observed these birds on the treeless Actaeon Islands. In fact, they nest in hollows in small trees in Tasmania during the summer months and lay 4–6 eggs in a clutch. The male feeds his partner while she incubates the eggs for 20–21 days. Chicks can fly at 4–5 weeks in time for migration to the mainland in Mar–Apr.

PREDATORS & THREATS: Clearing of habitat, predation by cats and raptors, and death during migration are all further endangering this bird.

Above: Feeding occurs at dawn and dusk, after which time they take to the roost.

DIET: Seeds; succulent plants
HABITAT: Salt marsh, sedgeland, fens, moors and buttongrass swamps

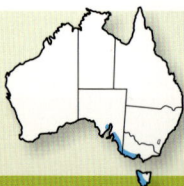

LENGTH: 20–22 cm
VOICE: A mellow tinkling sound in flight or a buzzing "zzt-zzt-zzt-zzt"
STATUS: Critically Endangered

Above: Such a good view of the orange belly feathers is rarely achieved.

Blue-winged Parrot *Neophema chrysostoma*

Many of the "grass parrots" share similarities in plumage at first glance. In areas where their ranges overlap, the Blue-winged Parrot could easily be mistaken for the slightly squatter Rock Parrot or the Elegant Parrot — both of which share its mostly yellow-green colouring.

FEATURES: A sunny yellow underbelly becomes golden-olive on the upper back and chin. Dark blue shoulder patches are larger and darker coloured than those on any of the similar grass parrot species in this genus. Males have a blue band at the top of the beak, but this is absent in juveniles and much paler on females. The shoulder patches of females and offspring are a paler blue-green.

DIET & HABITAT: Eucalypt woodlands and adjoining grasslands, as well as alpine grasslands, agricultural farmlands, Mulga, saltbush, spinifex country and coastal dunes, make up the chosen habitats of this diverse species. Blue-winged Parrots are ground-feeders that peck at seeds and herbaceous plants.

BEHAVIOUR: Blue-winged Parrots migrate north in autumn (some as far as Lake Eyre and south-eastern Queensland), with most returning to Tasmania in spring in anticipation of the summer breeding season. When feeding they are quite tolerant of humans and will allow intruders to come quite close before taking off with a short "tsit-tsit" warning call.

BREEDING: Blue-winged Parrots often choose stumps and logs for hollows, as well as orthodox hollows in tall trees. For about twenty days, the female incubates a clutch of 4–6 eggs, leaving the hollow a few times a day to be fed by the male on a nearby perch. Both sexes care for the offspring, which fly at 4–5 weeks.

PREDATORS & THREATS: Foxes, Dingoes, feral cats and habitat-clearing are the major threats to this species.

Left: A Blue-winged Parrot, when viewed from behind, displays the deep royal blue outer wing coverts for which it received its common name.

DIET: Seeds and herbs
HABITAT: Diverse; Mulga, saltbush, spinifex, farmlands, coastal dunes

LENGTH: 20–22 cm
VOICE: Tinkling, high-pitched squeaks of "tsiwee-tsiwee-tsiweet"
STATUS: Secure

Two distinct populations of this species exist on either side of the Great Australian Bight — one in Western Australia and the other in south-eastern South Australia extending into New South Wales and Victoria. Elegant Parrots are frequently confused with the Blue-winged Parrot, particularly in areas where their ranges overlap and especially when they flock together in winter feeding grounds.

FEATURES: Plain golden to olive plumage with few distinguishing markings save the blue band that runs behind the beak to the eye. The outer wing is also blue. The underbelly is a sunny yellow, developing to orange on some older individuals. Females are slightly duller than the males, with a less apparent blue facial bar. The facial bar is entirely absent on juveniles.

DIET & HABITAT: Usually this species lives in sparsely treed habitats on the edges of forests and woodlands, saltbush plains and even some coastal sand dunes. Semi-cleared farmlands and timbered grasslands, as well as riverine woodlands, are prime habitat for these ground-feeding seed-lovers. They also feed on some herbs and on saltbush, bluebush, fruit, berries and insects. Some Western Australian birds have been recorded in dense Jarrah forests of the South-West.

BEHAVIOUR: Elegant Parrots are sociable and may fly in large flocks. During breeding season they are mostly seen in pairs. They are not considered a timid species and often do not take off at first approach. When the flock does depart, it is usually rapidly, rising quickly into the air and flying quite high.

BREEDING: In the inland, nest hollows may be rather low, but they prefer very high hollows in their coastal range. A clutch of 4–5 eggs is laid and incubated by the female for 18–19 days. Males feed the female during brooding, and provide for the chicks for five weeks.

PREDATORS & THREATS: Feral cats, foxes and birds of prey will eat Elegant Parrots. Land clearing removes habitat.

Above: This is one of the plainest grass parrot species with few distinguishing features, although the blue on its wings is less royal blue (like the Blue-shouldered Parrot) and more aqua.

DIET: Seeds, herbs, some fruit, berries and occasionally insects

HABITAT: Diverse; usually sparsely timbered grasslands

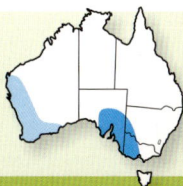

LENGTH: 22–23 cm

VOICE: Generally quiet but calls with a "chwit or "tzit" squeak

STATUS: Secure

Making the most of habitat that is under utilised by other Australian parrots, the Rock Parrot is a coastal bird, which prefers to live and breed on low limestone and sandstone cliffs directly by the ocean — a fact reflected in its species name, petrophila, *which is Greek for "rock lover".*

FEATURES: This species is the least colourful of all Australian parrots — plumage that is practical for camouflage in environments also frequented by predatory seabirds. The upper side of the body is a dull olive-green to brown, with brown, blue-fringed flight feathers on the wings and a yellow underbelly that graduates to green-brown at the neck. A blue band above the beak also encircles the eye, but is absent in juveniles.

DIET & HABITAT: Two distinct populations occupy the coastal dunes and heath of the southern Australian coast in South Australia and Western Australia. Rock Parrots also thrive on some of the mainland's offshore islands, such as Rottnest Island and Kangaroo Island. Succulent plants, coupled with the seeds of a few *Myoporum* species, comprise most of their diet.

BEHAVIOUR: Timid by nature, small flocks form to feed and, if flushed out of undergrowth, depart with a series of tinkling calls. Migration between the mainland and islands occurs in larger flocks, usually flying swiftly and sometimes making a return journey on the same day to roost on the islands.

BREEDING: Empty seabirds' nest tunnels, crevices in cliff-faces and depressions under coastal overhangs close to the sea's spray protect the 4–5 eggs of the Rock Parrot. Females lay from Jul–Jan and incubate the clutch for about nineteen days, all the while being provided for by the male. At 4–5 weeks, the offspring fledge.

PREDATORS & THREATS: Little Falcons are known predators of Rock Parrots. Increasing human populations in coastal areas could also threaten some nest sites.

Above: Rock Parrots appear shorter and plumper than most other *Neophema* species.

DIET: Seeds and succulent plants
HABITAT: Coastal dunes and heathlands

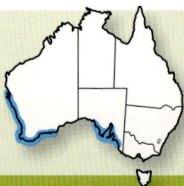

LENGTH: 21–23 cm
VOICE: Tinkling "tsee, tzit-tseit"
STATUS: Secure

Above: Camouflaged within the foliage of coastal heath.

Once teetering on the brink of extinction in the early 20th century, the Turquoise Parrot is a rare example of an endangered species making a remarkable comeback. The decline in their numbers was probably due in part to competition with plaguing rabbits, which fed on the same grasses from which these birds take their seeds.

FEATURES: In keeping with its name, the face of this parrot is an exquisite turquoise, with the female distinguished by the white lores above her beak. The central tail feathers are green, as is the back, with a bright scarlet band on the inner-wing coverts above a blue-violet shoulder. Both sexes have a bright, sunny yellow underbelly.

DIET & HABITAT: Either pristine or partly cleared woodlands and open grasslands suit this species, which is also occasionally seen on coastal plains. It particularly favours areas where rocky outcrops are interspersed with grassy plains and woodlands, such as near the Warrumbungles in New South Wales. Turquoise Parrots forage for seeds in understorey grasses. Paspalum, sorghum and the seeds of some introduced weed species are favoured.

BEHAVIOUR: This is another unobtrusive grass parrot, often unnoticed unless it is flying. They may move nomadically from one region of suitable habitat to another, crossing thicker forest. Most live in small groups of around seven individuals.

BREEDING: Low hollows in a fence post, log or trunk of a dead tree are the Turquoise Parrot's choice for nesting. When environmental conditions are favourable, they may breed twice during the Aug–Dec season. Two to six eggs are laid in a clutch. Fledglings vacate the nest at about 4–5 weeks.

PREDATORS & THREATS: Foxes, feral cats, Dingoes and interference with eggs are threats. Competition for food with introduced animals, such as rabbits and livestock, is also detrimental.

Above: An older female showing the orange belly feathers that appear on aged birds, leading to some mistaking them for Orange-bellied Parrots.

DIET: Seeds from grasses and shrubs

HABITAT: Woodlands and open grasslands

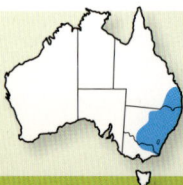

LENGTH: 19–21 cm

VOICE: A weak but melodius "tzeit-tzeit-tzeit"

STATUS: Rare but Secure

Above: Males have entirely blue faces.

A close relative of the Turquoise Parrot, this "splendid" bird inhabits drier terrain across the southern centre and inland. In the early 1900s, populations were believed to be in serious decline. However, by the 1930s, scientists had discovered that populations experience boom and bust cycles, breeding prolifically in good conditions to rapidly increase their numbers — a process known as "irruption".

FEATURES: Males of this species are some of the continent's most colourful birds, rivalled only by a few lorikeets. Their bright orange-red chest feathers contrast dramatically with a two-toned blue face, yellow underbody and green back. Females are plainer and attired in the green-yellow and blue feathers found throughout much of this genus.

DIET & HABITAT: Scarlet-chested Parrots are superbly desert-adapted. They are believed to obtain moisture from dew or by chewing on water-storing plants. A highly nomadic lifestyle allows them to move with the availability of water and seeding grasses in the arid and semi-arid interior of the continent. Their preferred environments are eucalypt, she-oak, Mulga, mallee, spinifex and saltbush woodlands. Most of their feeding occurs on the ground, where they seek seeds and herbs under the cover of shrubs, or in the understorey where their bright colours are less easily detected.

BEHAVIOUR: During population irruptions, flocks of around 100 birds have been sighted, but Scarlet-chested Parrots mostly live in pairs or small parties. In the wild, this is a docile, rather silent species that makes a gentle twittering "toowheet" or "chweet" call.

BREEDING: Breeding takes place from Aug–Dec, but during good conditions and following rain this species may breed several times. Females incubate 4–6 eggs on wood dust and shavings in a tree hollow for 18–21 days. Fledglings remain in the hollow for 28–32 days.

PREDATORS & THREATS: Predation by birds, feral cats, and foxes could impact on this species. They are probably more numerous in captivity than in the wild.

Above: Females are more drab in colour and could be mistaken for other parrots in this genus.

DIET: Grass seeds and herbs
HABITAT: Arid and semi-arid grasslands, spinifex woodlands, Mulga and mallee

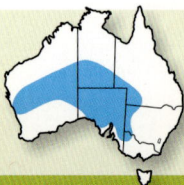

LENGTH: 18–21 cm
VOICE: "Toowheet", "chwit" or "chweet"
STATUS: Secure

Above: Despite the males' bright colours, these birds' behaviour renders them quite inconspicuous.

Blue Bonnets have no close relatives among the continent's other typical parrots and are the sole members of their genus. Characteristic differences are its somewhat pointed flight feathers and minuscule vestigial crest — features unique to this species among Australian parrots. Four subspecies are recognised — pallescens, haematogaster, haematorrhous and narethae.

FEATURES: The Blue Bonnet is typified by the deep blue face and forehead, for which it received its common name. The rest of the body is rusty red-brown, (slightly darker for the *haematorrhous* race, the Red-vented Blue Bonnet, which is the most colourful) with yellow lower belly and red around the legs and under the rump, depending on the species. The wings of all subspecies are olive-gold with blue and scarlet. The Red-vented Blue Bonnet has green on the tips of the shoulders.

DIET & HABITAT: Fruit, berries, seeds and nuts are the major components of the Blue Bonnet's diet. The four subspecies combined cover a wide distribution in the south-eastern States, with *narethae* alone existing in Western Australia. Much of this area is timbered grassland of Mulga, mallee, casuarina and riverine eucalypt. They are ground-feeders that mostly eat seeds but occasionally take nectar and native fruit.

BEHAVIOUR: Blue Bonnets appear to be able to do without water for some time, deriving most of their moisture from succulent plants and dew in arid areas. Where water is available, they drink at dusk and dawn and roost during the heat of the midday sun.

BREEDING: Mating follows rainfall in the inland but is mostly Aug–Jan. A low hollow is chosen and 4–6 eggs are laid. The female broods for 22 days, and is provided for by the male. Fledglings depart the nest at 4–5 weeks.

PREDATORS & THREATS: Birds of prey, land clearing, foxes, feral cats and Dingoes affect this species.

Above: The patchy red belly feathers of the *haematorrhous* race.

DIET: Seeds, berries, fruit and nuts

HABITAT: Diverse; timbered grasslands, Mulga, mallee and riverine woodlands

LENGTH: 27–34 cm

VOICE: Nasal and squawking "chzak-chzak-czakczakczak"

STATUS: Secure

Above: The supposed "blue bonnet" of this species is at the front rather than the back of the head.

Night Parrot *Pezoporus occidentalis*

One of Australia's most elusive and intriguing birds, this little-studied species has a lifestyle more akin to pheasant or quail species than to parrots. It shares its genus with the Ground Parrot, which also hides, feeds and nests in grasslands. So unobtrusive and rare is the Night Parrot that it was widely regarded as extinct for almost half a century until Australian Museum ornithologist Walter Boles found one dead by the roadside in 1990. Despite this find and subsequent unverified reports, many ornithologists believe this bird is likely to have succumbed to extinction. Most information about it is from 19th-century records.

FEATURES: Squat, dumpy and thickset, this parrot is very different to the colourful arboreal parrots. Its speckled green, yellow and black-brown plumage affords excellent camouflage in its environment. Both sexes are reported to look alike.

DIET & HABITAT: The Night Parrot occupies remote habitat in the spinifex country of central Australia, where it is believed to subsist almost entirely on the seeds of *Triodia* species.

BEHAVIOUR: By day, it is thought to hide in tunnels or runways in the spinifex and tussock grass. Early reports suggest that, when disturbed, it flushes from the undergrowth with an erratic flight pattern.

BREEDING: Information on breeding comes from historical sources. Reports surmise that it breeds after rain and nests in a similar way to the Ground Parrot — in loosely constructed tunnels inside spinifex or tussock grasses. Clutches have been recorded as having 2–5 white, oval-shaped eggs.

PREDATORS & THREATS: Damage to habitat and water supply by the introduced camel and domestic grazing animals, coupled with predation by foxes and feral cats, is thought to have played a part in this bird's decline.

Above: Despite best attempts to locate a living specimen, the Night Parrot, depicted here by artist Neville Cayley, remains elusive and is probably extinct.

DIET: Seeds, particularly spinifex seeds

HABITAT: Arid and semi-arid spinifex grasslands

LENGTH: 22–24 cm

VOICE: Said to be an extended, double whistle or a croak

STATUS: Critically Endangered, possibly Extinct

Ground Parrot *Pezoporus wallicus*

Ground Parrots represent an important exception to the other typical parrots in that they build their own nests on the ground (although Night Parrots may also do this). Two recognised subspecies of the Ground-Parrot — wallicus and flaviventris — inhabit a limited area along the south-eastern coast of the mainland from South-East Queensland around to the South Australian border, and in Tasmania.

FEATURES: The Ground-Parrot is similarly plumed to the Night Parrot, although slightly longer and more streamlined. The body colour is a deep green, heavily speckled with black and becoming yellow on the underparts. When the wings are spread, a yellow band is obvious over the top of the wing. The tail is long, with yellow outer tail feathers.

DIET & HABITAT: Ground Parrots are highly specialised coastal heath dwellers; however, they are occasionally found in swamplands and nearby grasslands. In Tasmania they are especially suited to button-grass swamps. They are seed eaters that survive on small seeding plants.

BEHAVIOUR: These are timid, retiring birds that are difficult to flush from the undergrowth, but when uncovered will flap erratically in a zig-zag motion for just a short distance before again going to ground and hiding. They are more often heard than seen, giving a high-pitched whistling call at dawn and dusk from the shelter of undergrowth.

BREEDING: Loose bowl-shaped nests are made of thin twigs and grasses. They are well-hidden in clumps of sedge, tall grass or heath shrubbery. Often the nest is accessed by a runway in the dense heath vegetation. Females lay 3–4 eggs and brood for 21–24 days. Offspring stay in the nest for 3–4 weeks.

PREDATORS & THREATS: This bird was once hunted as game, which probably led to its decline. Fire is a persistent threat. Foxes and feral cats also contributed to its decline.

Above: In its natural grassland habitat, the Ground Parrot is exceptionally well camouflaged and is rarely seen. When alarmed, it flies with jerky, awkward movements.

DIET: Seeds
HABITAT: Coastal heath, swamplands and some grasslands and buttongrass swamps

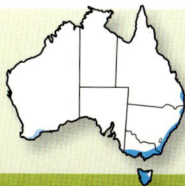

LENGTH: 28–30 cm
VOICE: Resonant whistles and trills as well as gentle twittering
STATUS: Considered Vulnerable in NSW

71

*Australia has a rosella representative for all States and Territories. Of them, the Pale-headed Rosella enjoys one of the largest distributions, with two subspecies (*palliceps* and *adscitus*) having a combined territory ranging from the tip of Queensland to northern New South Wales.*

FEATURES: A feature common to all rosellas is the scalloped effect of the back feathers. Colour varies widely, but all rosellas have these dark-edged feathers. As its name suggests, this bird is paler than its relatives. Its pale yellow head and back, coupled with varying breast and undertail feathers of blue and yellow (depending on the race) differentiate it from all other species. Race *palliceps* is almost entirely blue from the neck down, while *adscitus* has a blue band under the chin, a yellow breast and blue lower belly.

DIET & HABITAT: Scattered trees bordering agricultural lands, savanna woodlands, open forests with grassy understoreys, riverine woodlands and scrubby, sparsely treed ridges are its main habitat. Pale-headed Rosellas are primarily seed-eaters but supplement their diet with insects, nectar, fruit, flowers and flower buds.

BEHAVIOUR: Rosellas are active and sociable birds but can appear nervous around humans. Small flocks gather to feed but they are very often also seen in pairs, especially during the breeding season. Sometimes they form small flocks with Eastern Rosellas and are able to breed to produce hybrids

BREEDING: In drier regions they breed following rain, but the main seasons are Aug–Jan and Mar–Aug. Females lay 3–5 eggs in a high nest hollow and incubate them for 19–20 days. Males provide for the female while brooding and for the young chicks, which are fully fledged after about four weeks.

PREDATORS & THREATS: Illegal trapping, habitat destruction and predation by feral cats, foxes and birds.

Above: Northern populations in the race *adscitus* (shown here) have paler facial plumage than the southern race *palliceps*, which ranges south as far as northern New South Wales.

DIET: Seeds, insects, larvae, nectar and fruit

HABITAT: Savanna woodlands, open forests, sparsely treed farmlands

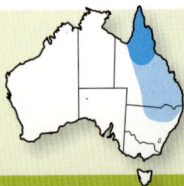

LENGTH: 28–32 cm

VOICE: "czik, czik" in flight but otherwise a mellow "fee-e-fee" or repeated "fwe-we"

STATUS: Secure

Green Rosella *Platycercus caledonicus*

The first scientists to describe the Green Rosella mistakenly thought the specimen was from New Caledonia, hence the erroneous species name caledonicus. *This is the resident rosella species of Tasmania and the Bass Strait Islands but it resembles juveniles of the mainland-based Crimson Rosella, to which it is actually closely related. Some ornithologists consider the King Island population of this bird to be the subspecies* kingii.

FEATURES: This is the largest rosella species and is sunny yellow on much of the body, aside from the black-fringed green back feathers, blue-edged flight and tail feathers, and colourful face. Males, females and juveniles all have a "beard" of blue under the beak and chin, and a crimson band above the beak. Juveniles are slightly greener overall than adults.

DIET & HABITAT: Common and abundant across most wooded environments in Tasmania. Green Rosellas are especially partial to the luxuriant mountain forests of high-rainfall areas. Like all rosellas, this species survives on a diet of seeds supplemented with insects and their larvae, nectar, blossoms and some fruit.

BEHAVIOUR: Green Rosellas are regularly vocal when in flight, making metallic "k-ziek, k-ziek, kziek" calls. When in small flocks, typical rosella behaviour is sociable and chatty, with flock members frequently twittering among themselves.

BREEDING: Even during the breeding season, this gregarious bird prefers to remain in small flocks. Nests are lined with woodchips and located high in the hollow limb of a eucalypt. Incubation of the 4–5 eggs takes 20–22 days. Although young fledge at five weeks, they remain dependent on their parents for a further 4–6 weeks.

PREDATORS & THREATS: Feral cats and birds of prey attack this species. As for most birds, deforestation and habitat clearing are a threat.

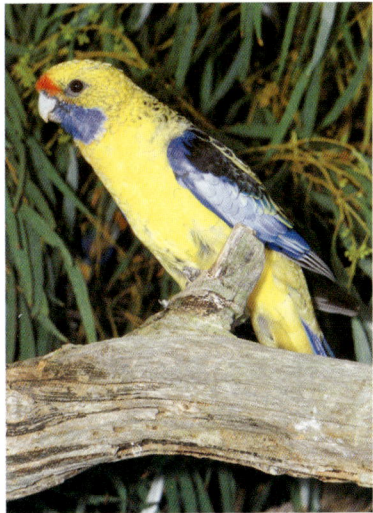

Above: Green Rosellas are gregarious birds that are frequent visitors to parks and gardens in Tasmania and the Bass Strait islands.

DIET: Seeds, insects, larvae, nectar and fruit

HABITAT: Most wooded habitats in Tasmania

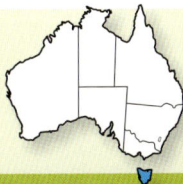

LENGTH: 32–38 cm

VOICE: Piercing triple whistle of "whee-whieit-whee" and a harsh "kziek, kziek"

STATUS: Secure

Four subspecies of this popular, friendly bird are found in Australia — all are frequent visitors to picnic grounds where they have become accustomed to humans. Race elegans *has the largest distribution. Race* nigrescens *is a north Queensland inhabitant. The two other subspecies, the Yellow Rosella (race* flaveolus*) and Adelaide Rosella (race* adelaidae*) were considered to be separate species and have common names that are used locally.*

FEATURES: Both males and females of the nominate race *Platycercus elegans elegans* are resplendent in crimson and royal blue with the characteristic scalloped back feathers and blue chin. Juveniles more closely resemble the Yellow and Adelaide Rosellas, with pale olive-green feathers and patchy crimson, blue and green. All races retain blue under the chin. The Yellow Rosella is distinctive for its lack of red plumage, aside from a small red frontal band above the beak. Speckled red-yellow plumage adorns the Adelaide Rosella.

DIET & HABITAT: Dense humid forests, rainforests, wet sclerophyll forests and timbered rivers and farmlands are the domain of the Crimson Rosella. The Yellow Rosella prefers riverine woodlands, belts of trees in agricultural lands and mallee. Adelaide Rosellas are mostly seen in dense forest and riverine woodlands around the Mount Lofty Ranges and the Adelaide Hills.

All feed on seeds, nectar, insects and some fruit.

BEHAVIOUR: During breeding season, males perform a fluffed-up, tail-wagging courtship display. Crimson Rosellas are gregarious and form small groups or flocks of up to 30 birds. They are easily enticed into gardens.

BREEDING: Nesting occurs from Sep–Jan in hollows in living or dead eucalypts. Females lay 4–8 eggs on wood dust and incubate them for around twenty days. At about five weeks, offspring leave the nest but remain dependent for 2–3 weeks.

PREDATORS & THREATS: Cats, Grey Goshawks and Peregrine Falcons are the major predators. Deforestation remains a threat.

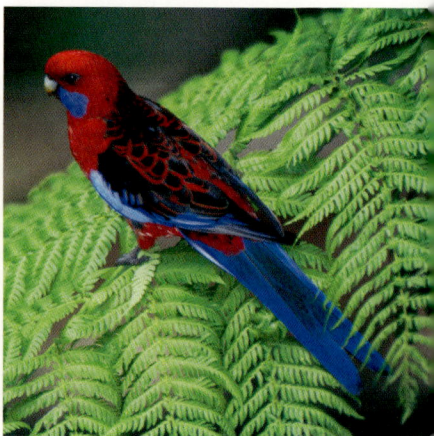

Above: The flamboyant Crimson Rosella, race *elegans*.

DIET: Seeds, insects, larvae, nectar and fruit

HABITAT: Diverse; riverine woodlands, open woodlands, rainforest, farmlands

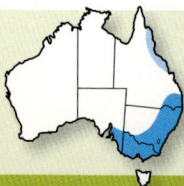

LENGTH: 32–37 cm

VOICE: A ringing "k-tee-tip, k-tee-tip", with the tee very high pitched

STATUS: Secure

Above, clockwise from top: Enjoying a bath; Adelaide Rosella, race *Adelaidae*; the Yellow Rosella, race *flaveolus*.

Some ornithologists refer to this species as the White-cheeked Rosella because of its obvious white cheek patches. Combined, the three subspecies — eximius, elecica and diemenensis—inhabit coastal and hinterland areas ranging from South-East Queensland to South Australia. The Pale-headed Rosella, which can hybridise with the Eastern Rosella in some areas, is sometimes also considered a subspecies of this bird.

FEATURES: The most apparent feature is the white cheek patch, which stands out boldly against the otherwise crimson facial feathers. The rest of the body is yellow, with black-edged feathers on the back and scarlet beneath the base of the tail. The wings are blue, as are the outer tail feathers. Females and juveniles are often slightly greenish in body colour.

DIET & HABITAT: This species enjoys a diversity of habitats, but prefers sparsely timbered woodland and farmlands, often with a grassy understorey, riverine woodlands and parks and gardens. It is usually not found at altitudes higher than about 1200 m.

BEHAVIOUR: They are mostly observed in pairs or small groups, which chatter continuously. Like most rosella species, they are sociable and bold, frequently approaching humans where they have become accustomed to receiving hand-outs at picnic grounds and parks.

BREEDING: Hollows are usually narrow and high in a tree limb, although sometimes stumps or logs are used. Most clutches contain 4–5 eggs, but as many as eight have been recorded. For 19–20 days the female incubates while the male supplies her with food. Offspring vacate the nest at five weeks.

PREDATORS & THREATS: Degradation of habitat and loss of hollows affect distribution and breeding respectively. Most predation is by cats, foxes and birds of prey.

Above: A female at the entrance to a nest hollow.

DIET: Seeds, insects, larvae, nectar and fruit

HABITAT: Diverse; open woodlands, sparsely treed farmlands

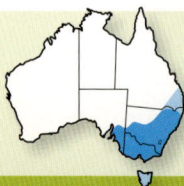

LENGTH: 29–33 cm

VOICE: A sharp, quick "whit-whit-whit" or a ringing "pee-pt-ee"

STATUS: Secure

Above, top to bottom: Males are highly distinctive and beautifully coloured; Shaking out the wing feathers after a bath has a kaleidoscopic effect.

*Restricted to a small patch of habitat in South-West Western Australia, the Western Rosella is one of the less commonly sighted rosellas and has two recognised races —*icterotis *and* xanthogenys. *It is the smallest species and prefers to live in pairs or small parties, rather than noisy flocks. Unlike most other rosellas, it feeds rather inconspicuously on the ground.*

FEATURES: Females appear much duller than males, which are almost wholly crimson on the underbody. Both have the sunny yellow cheek patches that are unique, among rosellas, to this species, although the male's is often brighter than the female's. The female's chest is a dull red with green mottling. Both sexes have green, black-edged feathers on the back, and blue on the upper outer wing.

DIET & HABITAT: Occupies an array of habitats, from tall, wet Karri forests to farmlands, semi-arid grasslands near the Nullarbor, and eucalypt woodlands of Salmon Gum. Fruit, berries and flowers are large components of its diet, but it will also eat insects and, of course, seeds, particularly of clover and casuarina.

BEHAVIOUR: More timid than most other rosellas. If alarmed they quickly retreat to the heights of a nearby eucalypt and survey the situation before flying further away. They feed quietly and make a gentle, tinkling "chink-chink" vocalistion rather than the noisy chattering of many other rosellas.

BREEDING: Hollows are usually about 5–15 m from the ground in a live or dead tree. For 19–20 days, the female broods her clutch of 3–6 eggs, receiving sustenance from her male partner. At about five weeks of age, the young birds are fully fledged and leave the nest.

PREDATORS & THREATS: As for most Australian birds, habitat destruction remains a threat. Most predation of this species is by raptors, cats and foxes.

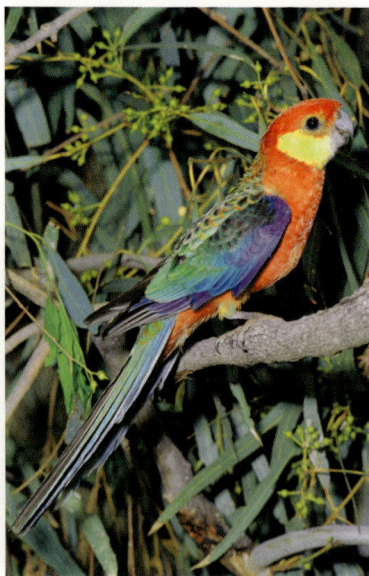

Above: The Western Rosella is the only rosella species to have yellow cheek patches, with the male's being slightly brighter than the female's.

DIET: Fruit, berries, blossoms, seeds, some insects

HABITAT: Diverse; semi-arid grasslands, wet Karri forests

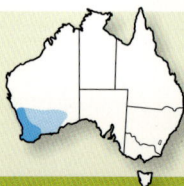

LENGTH: 25–33 cm

VOICE: A sharp, quick "whit-whit-whit" or a ringing "pee-pt-ee"

STATUS: Secure

This Top End version of the rosella is somewhat darker in colour than most of its relatives. It is also one of the least-studied rosellas, occupying remote environments where it has relatively small populations and rarely comes into contact with humans. Some ornithologists recognise a northern subspecies known as hilli, *which is said to have a larger bill and more violet in its cheek patch.*

FEATURES: The most obvious feature is the black "cap" on the top of the head and the greater amount of black on the body, including on the shoulder. The cheeks are white, often (in the north of the bird's range) with violet-blue. Except for the blue wings and tail, and a patch of crimson underneath the tail base, the rest of the body is yellow with a black scalloping effect.

DIET & HABITAT: Abundant eucalypt and melaleuca trees attract these birds to timbered open woodlands and grasslands and to tree-lined waterways. In these areas, Northern Rosellas search for seeds of trees, shrubs and grasses (melaleucas are special favourites), but also feed on flowers and some native fruit and berries.

BEHAVIOUR: In the cool of morning or early evening, groups of 5–20 birds feed on the ground, retiring to the shade of the treetops in the hotter part of the day. Tail-wagging and chattering,

typical of many rosellas, can reveal their treetop hideaway during this time.

BREEDING: Most breed from Jun–Oct, but the season may be extended from May–Nov. Hollows in trees near water are sought and 2–4 round eggs are laid. The female incubates the eggs alone for 19–20 days. The male brings food for her while she broods, but she leaves the nest briefly to eat at a perch. Both parents provide food for the offspring, which exit the nest at five weeks.

PREDATORS & THREATS: Populations may be in decline. Raptors, cats, Dingoes and foxes are the major predators.

Above: During the breeding season, these birds are mostly seen in pairs, although small flocks of 5–20 birds often gather to feed at other times.

DIET: Seeds, flowers, fruit and berries

HABITAT: Eucalypt and paperbark woodlands and grasslands

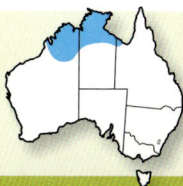

LENGTH: 28–30cm

VOICE: A sharp, "whit-whit-whit" and chattering in treetops

STATUS: Secure, but may be in decline

Species in the genus Polytelis *are often referred to as the "magnificent parrots", which is the Greek translation of their genus name — all of them certainly live up to this moniker. The Princess Parrot is sometimes also known as the Alexandra Parrot, after Princess Alexandra, the consort of King Edward VII, for whom it is named. It is one of Australia's daintiest, most delicately attired parrots.*

FEATURES: This elegant species is plumed in pretty pastels, and males are brighter than females. The male's chest, belly and crown are blue, while the chin and upper breast are flushed a lovely rosy pink. Females lack the blue underbelly of the males and are instead a dull yellow-green. The pink throat and the crown on the top of the female's head are also lighter, with the crown appearing more lilac than blue. The coverts of the primary flight feathers are blue from above and yellow beneath. Seen from beneath, the tail is a deep rose, but it is blue-green from above.

DIET & HABITAT: In the wild, this species occupies some of the continent's harshest environments. Bare areas of spinifex, sparse eucalypt woodlands, salt lakes, acacia woodlands and saltbush in the arid interior are its main haunts. Spinifex seeds constitute a large part of its seed-based diet.

BEHAVIOUR: Princess Parrots are elusive and strongly nomadic, forming small flocks that follow infrequent rains and seeding plants. Flight is slightly erratic and undulating.

BREEDING: Eucalypts or casuarinas, especially near water, often contain the hollows of several pairs of birds. Four to six eggs are laid and incubated by the female for around twenty days. Both sexes feed the chicks once they hatch.

PREDATORS & THREATS: So rarely seen are these parrots that nobody knows whether numbers are in decline. Many exist in captivity. Cats, foxes, Dingoes and raptors are likely predators.

Above: Males are splendidly attired in shades of pastel blue, aqua, rosy pink and green.

DIET: Seeds, particularly spinifex seeds
HABITAT: Arid spinifex land, salt lakes, saltbush and acacia woodlands
LENGTH: 35–45 cm
VOICE: Rather silent species but can make a loud "kee-ahrk-carruk"
STATUS: Vulnerable

Above: Females are as delicately coloured as males, but with shades of mauve where the male has blue.

Also named after a monarch, the Regent Parrot is more widespread than its relative the Princess Parrot, with two subspecies that live as separate populations on either side of the Great Australian Bight. The race monarchoides *is concentrated around the intersecting borders of South Australia, New South Wales and Victoria. Race* anthopeplus *is found in South-West Western Australia.*

FEATURES: Males are a brilliant yellow with olive-grey on the back and red-pink, blue and green wing feathers. The race *monarchoides* is generally brighter than *anthopeplus*. Females are, as usual, duller, being olive-green all over. The red on the female's wings is also duller than on the male's. The tail and wing tips are dark, with blue-grey outer tail feathers and primary flight feathers. In flight, the red wing feathers on the upper side of the wing are particularly apparent.

DIET & HABITAT: River Red Gums provide the most favourable nesting sites and consequently these birds often inhabit riverine woodlands or floodplains. Open forests and woodlands are also suitable environments. Acacia and eucalypt seeds make up most of their diet, but fallen fruit and nuts are also eaten by these mostly ground-feeding parrots.

BEHAVIOUR: They commonly live in pairs or in small, nomadic flocks. When flying, they communicate with a distinctive warbling vocalisation.

BREEDING: Males sometimes gift females with regurgitated food during courtship. Breeding takes place from Aug–Dec in high hollows in very old trees, often overhanging water. Incubation of a clutch of 4–6 eggs takes 21 days and is carried out solely by the female. Young Regent Parrots depart the shelter of the hollow at about five weeks but remain dependent on their parents for a further few weeks.

PREDATORS & THREATS: There are fears this species is declining due to the clearing of large, old trees in its habitat. Foxes, Dingoes, feral cats and raptors probably also contribute to decline.

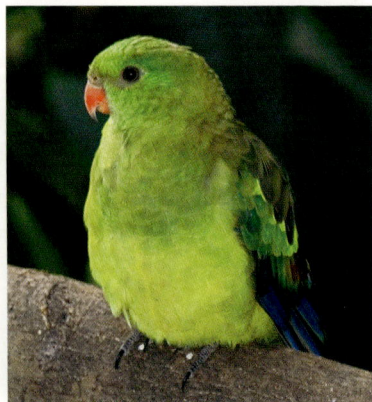

Above: The drab, mostly green plumage of the female (particularly of the *anthopelus* race) is in stark contrast to the male's sunny yellow.

DIET: Acacia and eucalypt seeds, fruit, nuts

HABITAT: Riverine woodlands, floodplains, open forests and woodlands

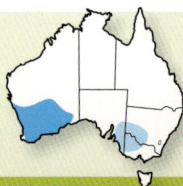

LENGTH: 38–40 cm

VOICE: A throaty and warbling "quarrak-quarrak-quarrak"

STATUS: Secure

Above: Race *monarchoides* has brighter yellow plumage.

Although once recorded in Victoria (with a range that reached almost to Melbourne), by 1938 naturalist Neville Cayley noted the Superb Parrot's extreme rarity. Now, the Superb Parrot is almost totally confined to New South Wales. Its decline is probably due in part to rabbit plagues and to the clearing of large River Red Gums, which are its preferred nesting sites.

FEATURES: Males are difficult to confuse with any other parrot species because of the sharply delineated scarlet-fringed bright yellow cheek patch, and patch above the beak. The eye is not enclosed. These markings, which are almost at right angles to each other, can give the male's head a boxy appearance. Females are very plain compared to the males, with almost entirely emerald green body feathers, just a patch of orange-red on the upper legs and a faint blue tinge to the cheeks.

DIET & HABITAT: Superb Parrots are birds of the riverine woodlands and forests, where they seek the sanctuary of large River Red Gums. They are commonly seen near the Murray, Murrumbidgee, Lachlan and Edwards Rivers. Feeding takes place on the ground in open grasslands and woodlands where they search for the seeds of native grasses and herbaceous plants. Grains such as wheat and barley also add to their diet, and they are sometimes seen on the road verge pecking up spilled grains. Superb Parrots will also eat psyllid lerps (the larvae of psyllid bugs, which are encased in sugary cocoons) and some nectar and blossoms.

BEHAVIOUR: Superb Parrots form small flocks that may be migratory.

BREEDING: Very high (20 m), deep hollows in River Red Gums are preferred. Females lay 4–6 eggs from Sep–Dec and incubate for 20–21 days.

PREDATORS & THREATS: Clearing of River Red Gums is highly detrimental.

Above: A male Superb Parrot stretches out in preparation for preening.

DIET: Seeds, grains, some flowers and nectar
HABITAT: Riverine woodlands, open woodlands and grasslands

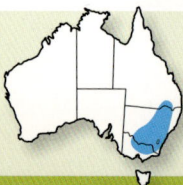

LENGTH: 37–42 cm
VOICE: Piercing but melodious "querr-ieek" or a squabbling "quarrrark"
STATUS: Vulnerable

Above: A young male, with the neck extended, shows the patch of crimson that appears ruff-like when fluffed up.

This extremely rare, endangered parrot exists in just one pocket of land on Cape York Peninsula. It was first recorded in 1858 and was known to have a limited distribution even then. By 1999, numbers were estimated at just 2000 wild individuals. The Golden-shouldered Parrot is also highly unusual in that it does not nest in tree hollows; instead, both parents work to excavate a tunnel in a termite mound.

FEATURES: Golden-shouldered Parrots are highly sexually dimorphic. Males are the more colourful and have a blue chest, red underbody, yellow shoulders and black back. The male's tail is green with patches of orange-yellow to scarlet under the base of the tail. Females are plainer in comparison and lack even the golden shoulders for which this species received its common name. Females are bronze-olive in the body with a pale, sky-blue lower belly and tail base and green upper tail feathers. Juveniles resemble females.

DIET & HABITAT: Golden-shouldered Parrots inhabit woodlands of paperbark and eucalypt that are interspersed with many termite mounds, especially conical ones. They sometimes also dwell in mangrove forests that fringe rivers. Grass seeds comprise most of the Golden-shouldered Parrot's diet.

BEHAVIOUR: They feed on the ground in pairs or small flocks and are not known to be shy, usually flying just a short distance if disturbed.

BREEDING: During the time that conical termite mounds remain damp from seasonal rains, both parents use their beaks to drill a tunnel and chamber at a height of 1–2 m. The female lays 4–5 eggs and incubates them for 18–20 days. Both parents feed the young for 4–5 weeks. Mounds are often reused in subsequent years. In good seasons, pairs may breed twice.

PREDATORS & THREATS: This bird is endangered, probably due to habitat destruction and fire.

Above: Males are distinguished from the similar Hooded Parrot by the red underbelly and by the fact that the eye is not enclosed in the black cap.

DIET: Mostly grass seeds

HABITAT: Paperbark and eucalypt woodlands and grasslands with plenty of termite mounds

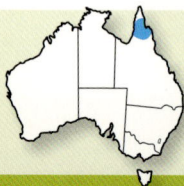

LENGTH: 25–26 cm

VOICE: Metallic but still quite melodius "chirrit, chirrit"

STATUS: Endangered

Above: Females are a much drabber green-blue.
A long tail is not ideal for a bird that nests in a hard,
narrow tunnel in a termite mound. Females that are
nesting can be recognised by their bent tails.

Hooded Parrot *Psephotus dissimilis*

Hooded Parrots have been, at certain times, classified as a subspecies of the closely related Golden-shouldered Parrot. When this species was first named in 1898, it was given the species name dissimilis *to indicate that it was considered separate or dissimilar to earlier records of the Golden-shouldered Parrot.*

FEATURES: Males are more boldly coloured than are the Golden-shouldered Parrots. They have turquoise bodies with scarlet only under the tail base. The entire eye is covered by the black "hood". Females are less easily discerned from their Golden-shouldered relatives, although are slightly paler with a yellow patch under the tail base.

DIET & HABITAT: Seeds mostly sustain these Arnhem Land birds, which prefer dry savanna woodlands and grassy, open forests with termite mounds.

BEHAVIOUR: Hooded Parrots are generally seen in pairs or small groups.

BREEDING: They breed from Apr–Aug, nesting in tunnels in termite mounds. Eggs are incubated for 19–20 days. The male feeds the brooding female.

PREDATORS & THREATS: Habitat loss, feral cats and fire are threats. Goannas enter mounds and eat eggs.

Above: Females (left) and males (right) form permanent pair bonds and prefer turreted-type termite mounds for nesting.

DIET: Mostly seeds

HABITAT: Savanna woodlands and grassy open forests with turreted termite mounds

LENGTH: 25–26 cm

VOICE: A sharp but thin "chsiet, chsiet" or a guttural, squabbling "charrak"

STATUS: Secure but rare

A victim of European settlement, the Paradise Parrot is presumed extinct. Its discoverer John Gilbert referred to it as "the most beautiful of the whole tribe I have ever yet seen in Australia", and its species name pulcherrimus, *translates as "most beautiful". Despite, or perhaps because of, the high praise this bird received, it quickly perished and the last records of it were made in 1927.*

FEATURES: Long, slender and colourful, it was presumably the male of the species that Gilbert and Gould were so enamoured with. With its green chest, turquoise cheeks, yellow-encircled eyes, red shoulder and salmon-coloured underparts, it was certainly a beautiful bird. Like the Golden-shouldered parrot, it had a black crown and black-grey back. Females were rather pale with grey-yellow heads, pale blue-green underparts and just a splash of red on the shoulder.

DIET & HABITAT: No-one is certain of the exact distribution of this vanished species, but it was thought to occupy a range from far northern New South Wales to as far north as Coen in Queensland. Grass seeds were known to make up most of its diet.

BEHAVIOUR: Very little is known about the behaviour of this species in the wild. It is believed to have lived a similar lifestyle to the Hooded and Golden-shouldered Parrots. Records do indicate that it probably lived in pairs or small family groups and was a ground feeder.

BREEDING: Like the Hooded and Golden-shouldered Parrots, it bred in termite mounds — generally low ones close to the ground. Records show that they bred in spring and summer and that brooding females were attended by the males. Both sexes probably helped raise the young.

PREDATORS & THREATS: Trapping for aviary birds, land clearing for grazing, competition with domestic stock and intentionally lit fires (to clear land for agriculture) most likely hastened the end for this unfortunate parrot.

Above: E.E. Gostelow's 1936 watercolour depicts the brilliantly plumed male Paradise Parrot (left) and less colourful female. Only a few specimens and artworks provide a link to this extinct species.

DIET: Mostly seeds

HABITAT: Grassy woodlands and scrublands with plenty of termite mounds

LENGTH: 27–30 cm

VOICE: Records indicate it made gentle, melodius whistles

STATUS: Extinct

*Two races of this species are accepted — *haematonotus*, of the continent's south-east corner, and *caeruleus*, which is found in more arid habitats around the Lake Eyre basin, where the borders of South Australia and Queensland meet.*

FEATURES: It is not difficult to guess why this species got its common name; however, only the males have red on the rump. The female's rump is olive-green. Both sexes are identified by the patch of white on the undertail coverts. Males have bright green-blue plumage on the head, becoming yellow on the chest, with a just a dash of yellow on the shoulder. The back is a darker viridian, except for the bright scarlet rump. Females are a plain olive-beige, becoming yellower on the belly and underside of the tail feathers. Juveniles have similar plumage to females. The race *caeruleus* is a little paler than the nominate *haematonotus* race.

DIET & HABITAT: Plains that are sparsely treed and grassy, as well as timbered waterways, mallee lands and farmlands, are where this species is most commonly seen. It is also frequently spotted in suburban areas, particularly around Canberra. The birds' diet is almost exclusively grass seeds, with some berries and leaves. Grit and sand is also eaten to help digest seeds in the gizzard.

BEHAVIOUR: Red-rumped Parrots live and feed in pairs or small flocks and are a sedentary, rather than nomadic, species. Pairs are affectionate and engage in mutual preening.

BREEDING: Breeding follows rain in more arid regions, but is mostly from Jul–Dec. A clutch of 4–7 eggs is laid in a hollow, usually in a dead tree or stump close to water, and incubated by the female for 18–20 days. Young Red-rumped Parrots stay in the hollow for 4–5 weeks.

PREDATORS & THREATS: This species has probably increased in numbers since European settlement due to more available grass seed and water. Cats, foxes and birds of prey are predators.

Above: Females are a nondescript olive-brown and do not have a red rump.

DIET: Mostly seeds; some berries and fruit
HABITAT: Lightly timbered plains, woodlands mallee and farmlands

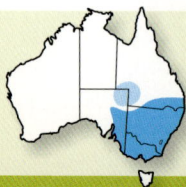

LENGTH: 26–28 cm
VOICE: A squeaky metallic "chwie-chwiep, chwie-chwiep"
STATUS: Secure

Above: The male feeds the female at the nesting hollow while she broods. The male's red rump is hard to see, except during flight.

Although closely related to the Red-rumped Parrot, the Mulga Parrot appears to have suffered adversely since European settlement while its relative has benefited. The male of this species is also known as the Many-coloured Parrot, for obvious reasons of plumage.

FEATURES: The male's green body is adorned with a red crown, yellow shoulder band, blue wing tips, yellow band above the beak and orange-red lower belly. Females are duller and lack the yellow shoulder and lower belly.

DIET & HABITAT: *Acacia aneura* (Mulga) scrub is just one of the favoured habitats of this bird, which is able to withstand drought throughout many of the arid woodlands across Australia's southern interior. Mulga Parrots also inhabit mallee and thickets of Cypress Pine. They dine on acacia seeds, seeding grasses and grain, which is often spilled by passing trucks. Mulga Parrots also eat some fruit, such as that of saltbush, bluebush and mistletoe, as well as some insect larvae.

BEHAVIOUR: They are unobtrusive parrots that form small, quiet groups and barely make any utterances at all when feeding. During drought, they move nomadically, seeking water and seeding grasses.

BREEDING: From Jul–Aug, female Mulga Parrots lay 4–6 eggs in a hollow in a tree near water. Incubation takes 18–20 days, and the male attends her while she broods.

PREDATORS & THREATS: The Australian Hobby is a known predator. Habitat clearing, cats and foxes are also threats.

DIET: Seeds and grains
HABITAT: Mulga scrublands, arid grasslands, saltbush and bluebush

LENGTH: 26–30 cm
VOICE: "Wit-wit-witwitwit" in quick succession and more gentle chattering
STATUS: Secure

Opposite: Despite its vibrant plumage, the male's emerald-green back camouflages it quite well when amongst grasslands. **Above:** A female about to enter the nesting hollow.

Although this species lives only in the South-West of Western Australia, it is quite abundant within its small range and is considered a pest by some fruit-growers, whose orchards are frequently raided. Despite its taste for fruit, this bird is highly specialised to exploit the seeds of the Marri eucalypt. While other birds have to laboriously gnaw through the Marri's thick, woody gumnut, the Red-capped Parrot's extra long, piercing beak is used to expertly scoop out the kernel with minimal effort.

FEATURES: This vividly plumed bird is so bright as to be almost gaudy. Males and females are similar, with distinctive scarlet "caps", brilliant yellow necks and sapphire blue on the belly, which becomes red on the lower belly and tail base. The back and inner wings are leaf green and the wing tips are blue.

DIET & HABITAT: This parrot occupies just a small territory in South-West Western Australia, where it is found across a range of habitats, from banksia heathlands to tall, wet eucalypt forests. The Red-capped Parrot's particularly long beak is specially adapted to enable it to prise out seeds from the seedpods of Marri trees. They also feed on other seeds, some flower buds, fruit, nectar, and lerps, but Marris appear to be a major component of their diet.

BEHAVIOUR: Many orchardists consider this species a pest, as juvenile birds often form large flocks that do considerable damage to fruit. Adult birds are less nomadic and tend to stay within their breeding territory all year.

BREEDING: From Sep–Dec, females lay in a hollow that is about 3–20 m high in a Marri or Wandoo tree. Each clutch contains 4–6 eggs, which are incubated by the female. During brooding, the male feeds the female on a perch near the nest. Both males and females feed the chicks, which leave the nest at 5–6 weeks of age.

PREDATORS & THREATS: Clearing of Marri could severely affect this species.

Above: In flight, the male's plumage is at its most spectacular with all colours on display.

DIET: Seeds (especially Marri), flowers and buds, fruit, nectar, lerps

HABITAT: Diverse; heath to wet eucalypt forest

LENGTH: 34–37 cm

VOICE: A warbling "kchurrink" in flight and a raspy rapid "chrrek" or "chirek-achek" in the trees

STATUS: Secure

Above: The long, sharply curved beak is specialised
for swiftly breaking into Marri seedpods.

Lorikeets

Lorikeets in the subfamily Loriinae comprise about 55 worldwide species. New Guinea is a major hotspot for lorikeet species. Australia, in contrast, has just six species of these vibrant birds, although the jury is still out as to whether the Red-collared Lorikeet (considered here as the *rubritorquis* race of the Rainbow Lorikeet) is a seventh species.

All lorikeets possess one special adaptation that makes them particularly suited for a diet of nectar — an absorbent "brush-tipped" tongue covered in fine, spongy protrusions that soak up nectar. This feature makes lorikeets especially crucial for the environment — as moving pollinators of dependent plant species. Lorikeets do not rely exclusively on nectar, but supplement their diet with fruit, seeds and insects. Unlike many other parrot species, males and females are almost identical and difficult to sex by sight alone. Even juvenile birds are very similar in colour to adults. Nevertheless, locating and discerning the opposite sex from other birds in the flock does not appear to be problematic for the lorikeets themselves.

Australia's species are distributed across much of the coast and hinterland of the continent, with the exception of a small pocket on the central coast of Western Australia. Flocks of lorikeets rarely go unnoticed, thanks in part to their kaleidoscopic colour, but also because they form extremely noisy groups that constantly chatter and squawk at each other. Some of Australia's best-known, most commonly seen bird species belong to the lorikeet family, including the ubiquitous Rainbow Lorikeet that so delights campers and picnickers.

Above: A Scaly-breasted Lorikeet feasts on a grevillea flower. **Right:** The aptly named Rainbow Lorikeet is one of the most common and most magnificent lorikeet species.

Musk Lorikeets, along with the other smaller southern species, are about half the size of most of Australia's other parrots. They were first recorded in 1789 in The Voyage of Governor Phillip to Botany Bay *and were given their scientific name in 1791. Their common name was bestowed due to the supposed, but unsubstantiated, musky odour of this bird when nesting.*

FEATURES: They are similar in green-brown body colour to the Little Lorikeet, but distinguished by their larger size, blue patch on the crown and red patch behind the eye — both of which are lacking in the similar Little Lorikeet. Females have a slightly paler blue crown. In flight, another feature is the patch of yellow on the underside of the flanks. The beak is also distinctive in having a dark base and a red tip.

DIET & HABITAT: Musk Lorikeets reside in open woodlands, forests, mallee, and cleared agricultural lands that have treed areas near watercourses. Nectar is the favourite food of this species, which is nomadic and follows the flowering of plants. Pollen, blossoms, fruit, insects and larvae are also consumed.

BEHAVIOUR: Musk Lorikeets often form small flocks with Little Lorikeets, Rainbow Lorikeets, Purple-crowned Lorikeets and Swift Parrots. They are nimble and noisy in the treetops, often dangling from branches and becoming very reluctant to move when engrossed in feeding activity.

BREEDING: Choosing a small hollow in a limb high in the treetops, the female lines it with wood dust and lays two eggs, which she incubates for 22 days. Unusually, the male joins the female in the hollow at night to roost. Offspring fledge at 5–6 weeks.

PREDATORS & THREATS: Cats, foxes and some raptors prey on Musk Lorikeets. Land clearing is a threat.

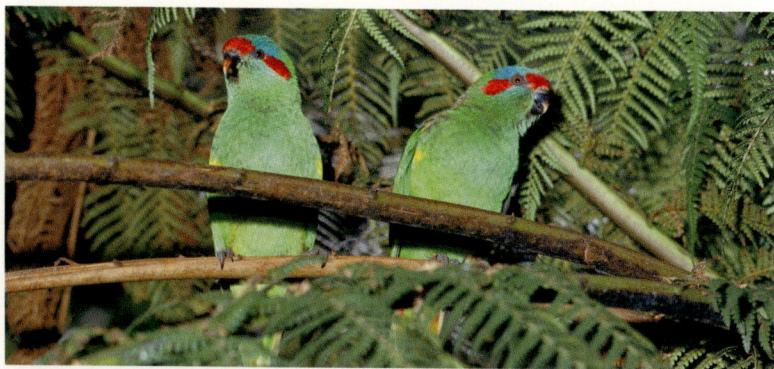

DIET: Nectar, pollen, flowers, fruit, insects and larvae
HABITAT: Open woodlands, forests, farmlands and mallee

LENGTH: 21–23 cm
VOICE: Piercing metallic shriek and chattering in the treetops
STATUS: Secure

Opposite: Even in a flock, permanent pair bonds of a male (right) and female (left) remain close together and are easy to spot. **Above:** A male feeding on a bottlebrush displays the characteristic beak colour.

Purple-crowned Lorikeet *Glossopsitta porphyrocephala*

Australia's second-smallest lorikeet species, the Purple-crowned Lorikeet is often heard rather than seen because its small size and muted colour allow it to camouflage remarkably well in the foliage. Usually, its hiding spot is only revealed by its noisy quarrelling and sharp "zit-zit-zit" calls, which have led to some people colloquially referring to this species as the "Zit Parrot".

FEATURES: Unlike some other lorikeets, juvenile Purple-crowned Lorikeets are much plainer than their parents and have just a hint of the mauve "crown". Adults are olive-green on the back and have wings with brilliant blue and crimson underwing coverts, a pale blue belly, yellow–orange cheeks and bar above the cere, a bright red spot near the eye, and the purple to violet-blue crown for which they are named.

DIET & HABITAT: Purple-crowned Lorikeets mostly prefer inland mallee and woodlands, but will visit flowering plants in coastal forests. They are also sometimes recorded in wet sclerophyll forests in South-West Western Australia. Nectar and pollen, mostly from the blossoms of hakeas, melaleucas, banksia, grevilleas and grass-trees, are supplemented by some orchard fruit, as well as insects and their larvae.

BEHAVIOUR: Purple-crowned Lorikeets are active, nimble birds that seldom come to ground. These lorikeets are nomadic and congregate in large groups where there are abundant flowering native plants. They have been seen gnawing on dry wood, probably to keep the bill in good condition.

BREEDING: From Aug–Dec, females nest in hollows in small inland trees or in high hollows in Karri forests. Each clutch contains 3–4 small white eggs that are incubated for seventeen days by the female. Once the chicks hatch, both parents provide for them until they leave the nest at 5–6 weeks of age.

PREDATORS & THREATS: Feral cats, foxes, fire and land clearing are threats.

Above: A male nibbles at seedpods.

DIET: Nectar, pollen, blossoms, some fruit and insects
HABITAT: Inland woodlands and mallee

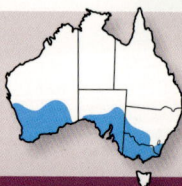

LENGTH: 15–16 cm
VOICE: Continuous "tziet-tiziet" or "zit-zit" in flight; soft chattering in treetops
STATUS: Secure

Above: Nesting pairs often breed somewhat communally, with the birds occupying every available hollow in a stand of flowering eucalypts.

Little Lorikeet *Glossopsitta pusilla*

As its name implies, this is the smallest of Australia's lorikeets and also the least colourful. It is also one of the most energy-efficient birds. Being small and swift, most lorikeets can obtain their daily nutritional requirements in just a few hours of feeding on sugary nectar. The rest of their time is therefore freed up to fly around seeking alternative sugar sources once their current food source expires.

FEATURES: Males and females look alike, with the only distinguishing feature on their otherwise emerald-green bodies being a "mask" of red on the face that surrounds the black beak but does not extend beyond the eye. In flight, the undertail coverts display orange-red at the base, which becomes yellow edged with green at the tips. Juveniles are slightly paler in the face and have brown irises rather than the adults' yellow eyes.

DIET & HABITAT: Open country is the Little Lorikeet's favoured environment, particularly where cleared or sparsely timbered land adjoins watercourses. They are opportunistic feeders that exist on nectar, pollen, fruit, seeds and berries.

BEHAVIOUR: These birds form fast-flying flocks of approximately twenty birds, although in winter and autumn, flocks of around 100 may gather to feed with the other lorikeet species that share their range. When feeding, Little Lorikeets can become very engrossed in their task and are quite approachable and reluctant to leave their feast.

BREEDING: Some hollows that are as low as 5 m from the ground are used, but they prefer to nest high in a live eucalypt that is close to water. Each clutch usually contains four eggs, but 3–5 are sometimes recorded. The female incubates the eggs alone for 22–23 days, during which time the male brings her food, which she consumes at the nest. Both parents care for the fledglings, which vacate the nest at around six weeks.

PREDATORS & THREATS: Cats, foxes, raptors and degradation of habitat are probably their biggest danger.

Above: Smaller than the Musk Lorikeet, with scarlet only around the bill, the sexes look alike.

DIET: Nectar, pollen, blossoms, some fruit and berries
HABITAT: Open riverine woodlands

LENGTH: 15–16 cm
VOICE: Short warbling shrieks of "zrrit, zrrit" or "chirrit, chirrit"
STATUS: Secure

Above: A brown iris, less uniform feathering on the body and an orange, rather than scarlet, facial mask all distinguish the juvenile.

The Varied Lorikeet's colourful speckled appearance lends it a unique attraction among Australian lorikeets. It is also the only lorikeet species to have a white ring around the eye, making it easily identifiable. Varied Lorikeets are the only Australian lorikeet in the genus Psitteuteles, *although there has been much ongoing debate about taxonomic classification.*

FEATURES: Along with the white eye-ring, the red cap is another feature unique to this lorikeet species. Males and females look alike, with green feathers streaked with yellow, pale blue, pink and red, and bright yellow cheeks. Young birds lack the bright red crown. Within its range, it is also the only lorikeet to have green underwings.

DIET & HABITAT: This species has the smallest distribution of the lorikeets. Dry tropical woodlands in the Top End, from Western Australia to the tip of Cape York, are their primary haunts. Pollen and nectar in the blossoms of bloodwood, paperbark and grevilleas are their favoured foods, but they will also eat insects and their larvae on occasion.

BEHAVIOUR: Varied Lorikeets are nomadic, moving with the flowering of bloodwoods, grevilleas and melaleucas. In the north-eastern parts of their range, they rarely form large flocks, preferring the company of only about twenty individuals. When in flight, these birds are particularly noisy, uttering repeated screeches.

BREEDING: Varied Lorikeets can breed year round but most breeding occurs from May–Sep. Hollows in trees along watercourses are favoured and are lined with woodchips, wood dust and sometimes bits of leaf. Eggs number 3–4 in a clutch and are incubated by the female alone for 21–22 days. The offspring remain in the nest for 5–6 weeks.

PREDATORS & THREATS: Foxes, predaceous birds, feral cats and habitat destruction affect this species.

DIET: Nectar, pollen, some insects

HABITAT: Dry tropical woodlands

LENGTH: 18–20 cm

VOICE: Rapid chattering when feeding; metallic screech similar to Rainbow Lorikeet in flight

STATUS: Secure

Opposite and above: Speckled feathering of gold threaded through green, aqua and rose body feathers, coupled with a unique white eye ring and red crown, makes this species unmistakable.

Scattered yellow plumage speckling the largely emerald-green chest feathers of this species gives it its "scaly" appearance and common name. It is closely related to the more colourful Rainbow Lorikeet and is able to form hybrids with its relative in some areas, although this breeding behaviour is the exception rather than the norm.

FEATURES: This is the only Australian lorikeet to have a totally green head — one of its defining features. Most of its other body colouring is on the underwing coverts and is only visible when the bird is in flight.

DIET & HABITAT: Scaly-breasted Lorikeets enjoy a diverse array of habitats along Australia's east coast, including woodlands near coastal heath, paperbark forests and anywhere flowering trees are plentiful. Populations are more abundant near the coast than in inland areas. Scaly-breasted Lorikeets are also frequently seen around cities and in suburban parks and gardens. Their natural diet is made up of nectar, pollen, native fruit, orchard fruit, seeds, sorghum crops and some insects, although studies reveal that eucalypt blossoms make up 71% of this lorikeet's diet.

BEHAVIOUR: This bird is nomadic, like all lorikeets, and frequently visits backyards to feed on native gardens and at birdfeeders. Scaly-breasted Lorikeets are gregarious and form small flocks, although in the breeding season they are most often seen in monogamous breeding pairs. They may also form flocks with Rainbow Lorikeets.

BREEDING: Breeding varies, with northern birds breeding from May–Feb and southern birds from Aug–Dec. A clutch of 1–3 eggs is laid on a base of wood dust in a high hollow. Incubation takes 23–25 days. In a good season, the female may brood twice. Both parents feed the chicks.

PREDATORS & THREATS: Powerful Owls are known to prey on this species. Dingoes, feral dogs and cats, and habitat clearing (in parts of its range outside of national parks and reserves) are major threats.

Above: Green interspersed with yellow on the chest gives a "scaly" appearance.

DIET: Nectar, pollen, fruit, seeds, crops and insects

HABITAT: Diverse; coastal heath, woodlands, paperbark forests, suburbs

LENGTH: 22–24 cm

VOICE: Rapid chattering when feeding; metallic sharp screech in flight

STATUS: Secure

Above: Flowering of native plants often attracts these birds to parks, gardens and backyards.

Rainbow Lorikeet *Trichoglossus haematodus*

The Rainbow Lorikeet is one of the most magnificent and engaging of all the continent's bird species. They are bold but welcome visitors to parks, backyards and campsites, where they descend in small, noisy flocks to be fed. Combined, two subspecies — moluccanus and the hotly disputed rubritorquis (which some consider a separate species) — inhabit coastal and hinterland regions from South Australia around to Cape York and the Top End. Another race, caeruleiceps lives on the Torres Strait island of Saibai.

FEATURES: The wholly brilliant blue head and lower belly are unique to this lorikeet species and make the Rainbow Lorikeet easy to identify. When combined with the emerald-green back, red and orange breast and yellow underwing band, this is truly a splendidly coloured bird. The Red-collared race is typified by a band of red, often speckled with blue, that runs around the nape of the neck.

DIET & HABITAT: Inhabits diverse environments, from rainforest to eucalypt forests, heath, mangrove forests and woodlands. This resourceful approach to habitat has allowed them to become very common. As well as nectar, Rainbow Lorikeets feed on seeds, fruit and berries.

BEHAVIOUR: Rainbow Lorikeets are popular attractions at sanctuaries and as aviary birds. They can be friendly around humans, and are often seen in city centres, but can be aggressive towards other birds when competing for food.

BREEDING: In the north, breeding is mostly from Mar–Jan and from Jul–Jan in the south-east. A clutch of 2–3 eggs is laid on wood dust in a high hollow, usually in a tree near water. Females incubate the eggs for 25 days. At 7–9 weeks, the offspring depart the nest.

PREDATORS & THREATS: Raptors, cats, foxes, Dingoes and dogs are threats.

Above: Some consider the race *rubritorquis* a separate species.

DIET: Nectar, pollen, fruit, seeds, fruit and berries
HABITAT: Diverse; coastal heath, woodlands, mangrove forests, suburbs
LENGTH: 26–31 cm
VOICE: Raspy musical screeches in flight, mellow twittering when roosting or in treetops
STATUS: Secure and common

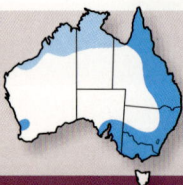

108

Above, clockwise from top: Feeding Rainbow Lorikeets at Currumbin Sanctuary; A breeding pair of the northern Red-collared race; Race *moluccanus* inhabits the south.

Glossary

ARBOREAL Tree-dwelling.

BARBULES Minute side hairs on a feather that interlock hooks with others to help form the flat surface plane of a feather.

CERE Fleshy skin at the upper base of the beak.

CLUTCH The number of eggs laid by birds and certain reptiles.

CORM A swollen, underground, food-storing organ of a plant.

COVERTS Small covering feathers in rows that conceal the bases of larger feathers.

DEFOLIATE To strip the leaves (foliage) from trees.

DISTRIBUTION Area(s) that an animal/plant naturally lives/grows in.

DIURNAL Active during daylight hours.

DOWN Soft feathers that first appear on young birds and also (for warmth) under the wings of adult birds.

ENDEMIC Native to a certain area and not found elsewhere.

EXTINCT Having no living examples of the same kind or species.

HERBIVORE An animal that eats only plants.

GENUS (PLURAL GENERA) A level of classification, one higher than "species". The first part of an animal or plant's scientific name is the genus. Different species can be included in the same genus.

INCUBATE To keep eggs at the right temperature for hatching young.

IRRUPTION An obvious, and usually rapid, increase in populations in a new area.

KERATIN A protein that is a major component of feathers, hair, nails, horns, and fingernails.

LARVA (PLURAL LARVAE) The young of any insect or invertebrate.

LORES The area between a bird's eyes and its beak.

MANDIBLE Jaw, or upper and lower parts of the beak.

MONOGAMOUS Having only one sexual partner at any time.

MOULT The periodic change of feathers: shedding of worn feathers and growth of new ones.

MUTUAL PREENING When two birds groom and preen each other's feathers.

NECTARIVOROUS An animal that eats only nectar

NOCTURNAL Active by night.

NOMADIC An animal or person that moves from place to place without a fixed home.

NOMINATE RACE The first-named race of a species (its race name will be the same as the species name).

OMNIVORE An animal that eats both plants and other animals.

POLLINATION Transfer of the male pollen grain to the female part of the flower; fertilisation.

PREEN Use of the beak to smooth and clean feathers.

POWDER-DOWN FEATHERS Special feathers, the tips of which break into flakes of keratin, which is used as a grooming powder.

PRIMARY WING FEATHERS The large feathers on the outer tips of a bird's wings, which are used for flight.

RAPTOR A bird of prey. The word comes from a Latin root which means "to seize and carry away".

SEXUALLY DIMORPHIC Difference in size, shape or characteristic between males and females of the same species.

SPECIES A group that shares the same physical features and can breed to produce fertile young.

ZYGODACTYLOUS An arrangement of toes, having two facing forwards and two facing backwards. From Greek: "yoke" + "toes".

Index

Publications

Cox, K. *Amazing Facts about Australian Birds*, Steve Parish Publishing, 2008

Currey, K. *Fact File: Australian Birds*, Steve Parish Publishing, Brisbane, 2006

Egerton, L. (Ed.) *Encyclopedia of Australian Wildlife*, Reader's Digest, Sydney, 2007

Egerton, L. *Know Your Birds*, Reed New Holland, Sydney, 2004

Forshaw, J. *Australian Parrots*, Lansdowne Editions, Melbourne, 1981

Higgins, P. *Parrots to Dollarbirds: Handbook of Australian, New Zealand and Antarctic Birds*, Volume 4. OUP, Melbourne, 1999

Kaplan, G. *Famous Australian Birds*, Allen & Unwin, Crows Nest, Sydney, 2003

Lindsey, T. *Green Guide: Parrots of Australia*, New Holland, Sydney, 1998

McNaughton, M. *Australian Parrots & Finches*, Bluestone Press, Victoria, 2004

Morcombe, M. *Discovering Birds: Brisbane & Surrounds*, Steve Parish Publishing, Brisbane, 2007

Morcombe, M. *Field Guide to Australian Birds*, Steve Parish Publishing, Brisbane, 2003

Links

www.newscientist.com

www.newsinscience.com

www.birdsaustralia.com.au

www.ausraptor.org.au

www.ausbird.com

www.absa.asn.au

www.iucnredlist.org

www.anbg.gov.au/birds/birds.html

www.austmus.gov.au/birds/stuff/bird_list.htm

Acknowledgements

The publisher wishes to thank Dr Les Hall for checking the facts contained in this book.

Published by Steve Parish Publishing Pty Ltd
PO Box 1058, Archerfield, Queensland 4108
Australia

www.steveparish.com.au

© Steve Parish Publishing

All rights reserved. No part of this publication may be reproduced, stored in a retrieval system, or transmitted in any form or by any means, electronic, mechanical, photocopying, recording or otherwise, without the prior permission in writing of the publisher.

ISBN: 978174193326 0

First printed in 2008

Principal Photographer: Steve Parish

Additional photography: Cliff & Dawn Frith/ANTPhoto.com: pp. 39 & 52; Graeme Chapman: pp. 7 (centre), 9 (bottom left & right), 25, 71 & 99; M & I Morcombe: pp. 5 (bottom), 7 (bottom), 9 (top right), 23, 29 (bottom), 37, 49, 57 (top), 62, 65, 90, 94-5 & 101; Ian Morris: p. 92; Night Parrakeet, Neville W. Cayley/National Library of Australia #an6952739: p. 70; Paradise Parrot, E. E. Gostelow/National Library of Australia #an3827575: p. 89

Front cover image: Crimson Rosella

Title page main image: Superb Parrot. Inset, top to bottom: Little Corella; Rainbow Lorikeets

Text: Karin Cox
Editing: Sarah Lowe, Les Savage; Michele Perry, Ted Lewis, SPP
Design: Lil Staff; Leanne Nobilio, Gill Stack, SPP
Image Library: Clare Thomson, SPP
Production: Tina Brewster, SPP

Prepress by Colour Chiefs Digital Imaging, Brisbane, Australia
Printed in Singapore by Imago

Produced in Australia at the Steve Parish Publishing Studios